# MENTAL HACKS TO RESILIENCE

# MENTAL HACKS TO RESILIENCE

Stress Proof Your Brain, Stay Successful,
Build A Resilient Mental Attitude Through
Classic Quotes And Success Principles.

**Maria C Vale**

From a successful business executive, now a Stage
IV Cancer survivor of 10+ years, who's used many
of these quotes not only to survive, but thrive,
despite all odds.

*To those of us who have fallen the proverbial seven times, ready to stand up the eighth.*

# CONTENTS

# MENTAL HACKS TO RESILIENCE

# INTRODUCTION

## About These Mental Hacks

There's no doubt that nowadays the world feels more chaotic, annoyingly unpredictable and quite stressful to control freaks like us. If you're the more enlightened type, using Zen methods and meditation to manage all that, I say kudos. If that works for you, awesome. But as you know, everyone is wired differently. And while some people use exercise, overeating, drinking, meditation, yoga, road rage, etc. to deal with it all, some of us hack our way back to sanity with the help of quotes, aphorisms, the wisdom of the world to keep us in line. We use the words of others who've experienced similar situations to keep us a little saner when dealing with daily challenges. In my case, these have become effective mental markers which have helped me along, year after year, through the good and the tough times, to remain focused and centered. I consider them my little mental hacks to resilience. Having these quotes pop up in your calendar is like having a personal coach, or a team of them, from times past, reminding us of what we need to do to achieve the levels of success they had.

If you are the kind of person who also collects quotes that resonate with you, then this book is for you. Of course, this is not just a simple collection of quotes. Here I am sharing how this timeless wisdom has helped me take a deep breath, a step back all while offering fresh perspectives in different situations of life. They reset me mentally and help me stay focused. I am hoping they do the same for you. Of course, the purpose of this book is not only to share but also to entertain you. So, while some of these reflections can come across as deep and serious, they will also contain anecdotes and other witty observations, which I hope make you smile.

## Why I'm Sharing This With You

Now, I don't consider myself a celebrity, or someone even close to being ultra-famous, ultra-successful, or ultra-rich. I'm your average Jane, working hard to make it in this world and leave my mark, just like you. I am as imperfect as they come, have daily temptations and challenges, and like all of us, sometimes I don't succeed. But I look to my little hacks to help me stay the course and achieve in the long run. I had a successful career in sales and business development, working for corporate America out of New York City. In my later years, life benched me from my profession due to serious and recurring bouts with cancer. I had to choose between doing what I had been doing or changing my life to survive. While that seemed like a daunting task, I managed to get it done. Currently, I consider myself early retired; I am alive and thriving despite my decade-old Stage IV breast cancer diagnosis. Of course, there are dozens of factors that have contributed to that unusually long survival. Resiliency and a determined mindset are just two of which I give credit. And these aphorisms, quotes, and sayings that I have kept at hand during my college days, and all throughout my career and various health challenges, have been my little mental hacks to stay resilient. Each one acting as a flashlight in the darkness of the scariest days or as reminders to enjoy the best moments. However much longer I have—which I hope is at least a couple more decades—I want to share with you what has kept me going day after day, in all aspects of life, and what has come in handy when dealing with life's challenges. My hope is they help you as well.

## How To Set Up A System Of Quotes To Keep You Motivated And Resilient

While it's fun to discover new quotes that resonate with us, it's a good idea to set them up in a system that keeps us motivated and gives us the necessary perspective to cut thru the mental noise and moving towards our life goals. Many years ago, during the early days of handheld devices, I discovered I could put them in my automated calendar. It was the mid-1990s, and I was thrilled at the magic of the recurring appointment. So, I started taking them off the post-its I'd been using and entering one per day as an event in my calendar, setting it up to recur year after year until the end of time (or at least until my cloud subscription expires). As I discover new ones, I add them into the rotation. Now, some of these quotes are so important that I set them up to recur weekly.

If you find quotes motivate you and give you that necessary perspective to make it through your day, this could be something you could also incorporate in your electronic calendar as a motivating system. If you prefer a more tangible version, then there is always the old way of little reminders written on color post-its stuck along whatever thing you look at often, whether it's the fridge door, computer monitor, or your bathroom mirror. It's important to have them present. If you're not sure how to set them up in your calendar as a recurring appointment or event, I have a free tip sheet that you can download from my website. You can find that information in the Afterword.

## How This Book Is Set Up To Help You

Mental Hacks to Resilience is divided into theme sections and subsections, to make it easier for you to find quotes and reflections relating to topics that address a particular issue of interest to you. As you know, sometimes we need a different perspective, something that tells us someone else has been in your shoes, that you're not alone in the situation. At the end of each section there is a page for notes so you can jot down your thoughts and make this book your own.

If you have your own quotes, or stories and reflections you'd like to share on your favorite ones, join me on social media. All that information will be available in the Afterword. I would love to hear from you, and how they help you. The idea is to get the world talking and thinking, about how we can use this timeless wisdom to guide us today, or at least understand things in a new way.

## What I Hope This Book Does For You

My hope is that in this book you will find not only a different perspective when dealing with your world, but also be reminded that we're all in this struggle together, that no one has a perfect life, and that we can find our own way to our personal definitions of happiness and success.

# SECTION 1:

## OUR RELATIONSHIP WITH OTHERS

The interactions we have with the people in our world can make or break our entire days (or lives, if you are feeling a bit dramatic). That smile from the barista who always calls you by name can turn a good morning into a great one. On the other hand, someone cutting you off in traffic and then making a rude gesture like it was your fault can make you want to throw the whole day away and start over. And those are just the strangers in our lives! We have our friends, our loved ones, our children, our parents, so many people who hold a chunk of our hearts and can influence how we are feeling.

It is always important to remind ourselves that while we can't control other people's actions, we can control our reactions. We are the only ones who hold the power to change our emotions toward the things they do. So, while I'd rather the world swallow me whole than have an awkward moment while trying to impress my manager in front of a client, all I can do is let go of the embarrassment and keep moving forward.

Each relationship we create is unique and defined by its own rules, not to mention how they are susceptible to change over time.

Our relationship with our parents differs greatly in adulthood from the one we experienced in childhood. Same as those with our own children. Every person you meet has the capability to become a close friend or loved one; the excitement is in never knowing which is going to happen. This section of quotes is intended to help you ease the stress of maintaining your relationship with others. The world loves to throw us challenges—like, oh, I don't know, let's say a global pandemic or something—that tests every single one of our relationships, and it is up to you to either flex with them or watch them snap. These quotes span a range of wisdom, from thoughts on expectations to career success, leadership, romance, etc.

I share with you my reflections and experiences to not only offer advice on how to deal with the various people we encounter on a daily basis, but also a validation of the fears and frustrations you may feel during social situations. There is nothing more reassuring than the acknowledgment of the collective discomforts we all experience as we fumble through this existence. That's what I'm here for, my new friends. Don't worry, I've got your back.

# On Those in Our Close Circle: Friends and Loved Ones

*If you expect great things of yourself and demand little of others, you'll keep resentment far away.*

— Confucius

I think this quote serves as a warning that perhaps we shouldn't place too many expectations on people in order to avoid disappointment. For example, it's okay for me to expect the person behind me to say, "Thank you!" when I hold the door open. It's not okay for me to expect A-list actor Chris Hemsworth to run into me at a Starbucks, fall instantly in love, and want to run away together.

A last thought on expectations: Expect the ones you love to let you down at least once in the relationship. We're all human; we make mistakes and misjudgments. We will also disappoint people. When it inevitably happens, will you be mentally prepared to forgive and move on, or will that one-time disappointment be the deal-breaker despite all the history and bonds?

*Relationships are based on four principles: respect, understanding, acceptance, and appreciation.*

—Mahatma Gandhi

Totally agree with this one. And it needs to go in both directions, otherwise there is no balance. Relationships require you to trust in another person to treat you the way you want to be treated; and for you to do the same. I'd say among the collection of quotes here, this one is probably the most important.

Out of the four principles listed in this quote, I find respect to have the most weight. It's true that when it comes to our families, sometimes respect can be set aside in the heat of the moment, but when the overall arc of the relationship is based on respect, that can be considered healthy. However, if respect is constantly missing from the relationship, it's time to give it some thought. When it comes to romantic relationships, I believe that respect is most important, but when attraction gets in the way, it can cloud one's judgment. I recall when I was 17 and fell head over heels for this hot looking guy. We dated for a few months but, as the relationship progressed, I noticed his temper would flare up and he'd call me names and insult me. What a quick way to help me get over him!

Suffice to say, his lack of respect for me slowly made me see past his good looks and move on. Don't get me wrong, it wasn't easy. When feelings are involved, walking away is tough, but your love and respect for yourself should be above all. If people you love don't treat you well, it's not a healthy relationship. I like my relationships how I like my house: stable and built on a good foundation. And preferably without any overwhelming smells.

*Kindness is the language which the deaf can hear and the blind can see.*

–Mark Twain

Kindness is the kind of thing that you can't see or touch, but you can certainly feel. It's in the tone of our voice, the way we look at someone, the way we stand before them, in the way we behave towards them, and it doesn't cost us a dime. So, while there are times when we are not inclined to be kind, let's remember that it's a gift we can give someone, and you can be sure it'll have an impact. Nothing turns your day around faster than a text from a friend when they see something that reminds them of you, or a treat from your brother, "just because."

I think kindness is the basic tenet of all successful relationships. Like toilet paper in a public restroom, when it's missing from your life, you definitely feel the loss. You'll find that being kind is a recurring theme throughout this book, and hopefully throughout your life as well. I encourage you to sprinkle it around so that it sticks in those hard-to- reach places, and you discover it again when you least expect it, like glitter in a kindergarten classroom.

*One should always play fairly when one has the winning cards.*

–Oscar Wilde

This one speaks volumes about who we are. Taking advantage of our close friends and family is a fast way to foster distrust and fracture our relationships. If we can't be fair with the ones we love, then are we really winning? And that ace up your sleeve doesn't count. Drop that poker face and show your hand; people will respond favorably to you when you aren't playing games.

For some reason, this quote takes me to the tough times in a relationship, when there's so much hurt and resentment that it's hard to play fair with that loved one. I've seen examples of break-ups between people who, at one point, were crazy about each other. And while it's likely all they have left is disappointment, I've seen how kind and fair actions of one toward the other save the relationship from drowning altogether. With time a friendship emerges, because even in the worst times there was fairness.

*It is one of the blessings of old friends that you can afford to be stupid with them.*

–Ralph Waldo Emerson

This quote brings back memories of college and childhood. God knows how grateful I am that there were so many wonderful people around who put up with me during my foolish times. They are the people who have remained true friends to this day, with whom I can still be silly regardless of how far we've come in our lives. Having those longtime friends who have seen me at my weakest, most embarrassing times yet still love, support and accept me as I am, humbles me and makes me feel so lucky.

I think back to my college days, and I can't help but laugh at the craziness we all shared, and be happy we can still sit together today to enjoy a meal and laugh at ourselves. I am sure you can think of a couple of people in your life who have that significant role. Hang on to those friends; they are a treasure. I always say that if you can't handle me at my 2 a.m. karaoke to the local 24-hour diner crowd, then you don't deserve me at my best.

*We have two ears and one mouth so that we can listen twice as much as we speak.*

–Epictetus

Amen to that. Relationships are a constant balance of give and take, and there are times when it is more beneficial to give. It's important for our friends and loved ones to feel as though we're listening to them and truly hearing what they are saying, rather than just waiting for our turn to talk. No doubt we've all been guilty of talking more than we listen. Guilty as charged here. But this quote is such a great reminder, and I can't help but think back to the people who took the time to listen because sometimes that is all I needed. Sometimes that is all our loved ones need. Who likes hearing the sound of their own voice anyway? (Forget I asked. I'm sure we can think of one or two people.)

*The greatest good you can do for another is not just to share your riches but to reveal to him his own.*

–Benjamin Disraeli

Another favorite quote, especially applicable to those deserving friends and loved ones in our lives. No doubt about it, it's nice to share our successes and our wealth with those we appreciate and love. Sometimes it might even be your goal in life to make enough money to buy a house for your parents or a new car for a sibling. Yet an oft- forgotten great gift is helping them discover how they can be as successful, in wealth and happiness, on their own terms. There's great joy in helping them find their path, perhaps capitalizing on their strengths, and motivating them to find that niche that will get them there. There are times when friends have even gone into business with one another, taught each other their successes, and prospered together.

There have also been times when they end up as competitors, which is why it is important to be discerning about sharing. Those are decisions that we need to make as we cross those bridges. I remember a very successful colleague during my days as a pharmaceutical rep, who once said, "I can teach you my best detail tactic and still beat you at it." Hearing her say that was a bit intimidating. She was certainly not afraid of sharing her skills with colleagues, who could become competitors. Talk about a high level of self-confidence. We can all aspire to that because it's people like her who make our world better (well, at least the business world).

*Two persons cannot long be friends if they cannot forgive each other's little failings.*

–Jean de La Bruyère

Another important aspect of relationships. I used to expect perfection from people, but as I got older I realized the sentiment behind this quote, and it's made things easier. It has also helped me to understand that I can't expect perfection from others when I am imperfect myself. The key question is, are we willing to forgive and look past those small imperfections? Of course, if those imperfections are consistently hurtful, then it's time to reconsider the trust in that loved one. But acceptance is the general rule when it comes to our loved ones.

*You don't develop courage by being happy in your relationships every day. You develop it by surviving difficult times and challenging adversity.*

–Epicurus

No doubt, all relationships hit the proverbial rocky road from time to time. Miscommunication, unresolved feelings and failure to meet expectations are common hardships that can occur in romantic, platonic and familial relationships. The question is, can we make it through? Is it worth the effort and sacrifice? Whether it's our parents, kids, siblings, spouses, friends, they can drive us crazy or disappoint us at times. Let your past struggles strengthen the person you are today. If every relationship were perfect, there would be a severe lack of innovation, creativity, and comedians. You get to choose how to define your past rather than letting it define you.

───────────────────

*Family not only need to consist of merely those whom we share blood, but also for those whom we'd give blood.*

–Charles Dickens

Or a green tea latte. Give me one of those, and we're family for life. And as popular as vampire fiction is these days, this quote is more along the lines of the "found family" trope. That ragtag group of misfits that we've collected along the way, who are there for us no matter what we are battling, and who can often feel closer than any genetic relation. In the unfortunate circumstance that those who are connected to you by blood fail to support you, the family we make for ourselves will always be there. And while you may never need them to help you stop Voldemort or Thanos from destroying the whole world, you'll want them around to help prevent you from ruining your own.

# Dealing With Our Children and Our Aging Parents

*We can complain because rose bushes have thorns, or rejoice because thorn bushes have roses.*

–Abraham Lincoln

Ole Abe is back at it again. This time with advice about your prickly child. At some point, we have to realize that we can only mold our children so far until their personality develops. I find that too much time lamenting the loss of the idealized child you've built up in your mind, only succeeds in shortening the time you have with the actual child in front of you: A kid full of thorns, roses, love and laughter. And maybe too many Pop-Tarts.

*Where parents do too much for their children, the children will not do much for themselves.*

–Elbert Hubbard

Oh! I can speak to that from first-hand experience. Growing up in Latin America, we had housekeepers. When my parents were divorcing, and things began to dissipate in my household, all the help we had begun to go away. The day the last housekeeper left, I remember coming home from school and seeing the beds unmade, the dishes still in the sink, no lunch ready, and the 10-year-old spoiled creature in me became indignant that the house was not in an acceptable state. I recall asking my mother what happened, in a demanding tone. When she told me good old Grace had left, I remember angrily asking her then who was going to do all that work? My mom pointed at me and said, "You are." I was so upset. I started crying.

Fast forward a few years later, as we arrived in the United States, we had to do everything for ourselves. Thankfully, I was already trained in that situation. But I look back and wonder, had I been raised all my young life with housekeepers, expecting things to be given to me by parental figures, what would have become of me? So, despite the unpleasant situations that led to that, I am grateful it happened. This quote couldn't be truer, and I'm just glad I dodged that bullet of growing up as a spoiled brat, who expected everything to be handed to her by parental figures. I was well on my way there.

Remember to teach your child to think about how they're going to take care of themselves, their surroundings, and succeed on their own. It's the best gift you can give them, over everything else you're killing yourself to ensure they have. Even more so than those new Nikes or one of those ring lights for TikTok.

*What we know is a drop. What we don't know is an ocean.*

–Sir Isaac Newton

God knows this is a reminder that we can never assume we will always be able to predict exactly how the ones we love will react or behave in certain situations. Chances are we might know, but there are those moments when they will surprise us. And that's humbling. I've gotten my proverbial wake-up moments with some of my loved ones and learned my lesson well. People will never cease to surprise you with their vices and virtues (or political preferences), no matter how well we think we know them. So, never assume you know someone so well that you can predict their behavior, no matter how close you are, or you'll be in for a humbling surprise, which is why I am a strong advocate of constant and open communication with those in our inner circle. The moment it breaks down, we can let assumptions trip us up.

*Educating the mind without educating the heart is not education at all.*

–Aristotle

Teaching a child how to excel in school without also instilling awareness of their feelings and behavior around others will hinder their ability to experience life to the fullest. What's more, not preparing our children for the delicate intricacies of human relations—friendships, love, heartbreak, dealing with authority figures who are hellbent on destroying them and their two best friends—by assuming they'll figure it out on their own, instead of giving them guidance, is as bad as not giving them a formal education.

Haven't you ever wished that schools had curriculums that addressed how to eat right, how to manage our finances, and how to navigate human relations? I know I have. We'd be better functioning human beings in our society. So, for now, ensuring our kids are well-versed in those aspects, especially when it comes to educating the heart, is still up to us.

A personal suggestion here: If you don't think you have the time or expertise to address the human relations front, I say go to the all-time expert, Dale Carnegie, and share his knowledge with your kids. I read his books when I was 10. They're still best-sellers today, especially How to Win Friends and Influence People, published in 1936, which has sold over 15 million copies worldwide, and continues reach millions of readers to this day (Simon & Schuster).

His books are permanently on my shelves, and I still read them from time to time. They had a huge impact because they taught me to be more aware of the people around me, to really see the world beyond my nose, and realize how our behavior can affect others. I am so grateful to my mother for sharing Dale Carnegie with me. I am sure many of you reading this book know well what I'm talking about. And if you don't, I invite you to look him up. It'll be worth your time. That's one education no academic curriculum can teach.

*Experience is the teacher of all things.*

–Julius Caesar

Whether we adore our parents (or hope that a strong wind will come to carry them away), we have to acknowledge that their life experience can still be great guidance for us. If we're very lucky—and if they're still around—we can count on them to help us through the situations that they've seen before.

I feel like each year I relearn the fact that my parents are just people too. The more life experience I acquire, the more I realize that no one is omniscient. You can still turn to them with all your questions but do it with the understanding that they won't have all the answers. Alas, will any of us ever learn how to fold a fitted sheet?

*Patience is bitter, but its fruit is sweet.*

–Aristotle

The main reason for having this quote here is to relate how sometimes we need to take a deep breath, collect our thoughts, and just let a situation be. It's about picking our battles with our children and parents in order to maintain the overall balance of the relationship.

There is certainty in the fact that we will encounter areas of disagreement in how we approach different situations, and there are times when we just have to let them take the lead, even if we know they're wrong, as long as they don't hurt themselves. Sometimes you really have to remember how sweet the fruit of patience is when it comes to dealing with the ones we love. Almost citrusy, right?

*I hear and I forget. I see and I remember. I do and I understand.*

–Confucius

While this quote applies to many aspects of life that involve other people, I share it in this section because our children and parents are usually the ones closest to us. They need to understand us, and our situations, the most. So, don't just tell, show. And, even better, get them involved.

# Dealing With Difficult People and Differing Opinions

*Nothing can stop the man with the right mental attitude from achieving his goal; nothing on earth can help the man with the wrong mental attitude.*

–Thomas Jefferson

I find this quote to be equal parts encouraging and frightening. Encouraging in the first half and frightening in the second. In addition, the second part is a sobering truth when dealing with difficult people, especially when those who are stuck in a certain mindset will close their ears and barrel forward toward what they believe is the truth.

And while a perfect world would see every person we meet as falling within the first category of this quote, unfortunately, we're still waiting on that utopia; because there are a fair amount of people who fall in the second. Nothing on Earth, eh? Perhaps that's what the missions to Mars are for.

*Kindness is in our power, even when fondness is not.*

–Samuel Johnson

This goes back to starting with kindness first. It is an admirable feat of strength to be a genuinely kind person in the face of someone who is not. Every interaction we have is going to be different, and some might lean more toward the uncomfortable end of the spectrum. But you can always kill them with kindness! (Because killing them with anything else would just be murder... and that's a no-no.)

***

*Wise men speak because they have something to say; fools because they have to say something.*

–Plato

Remind you of anyone in those company meetings? The coworker who mansplains everyone else's answers or the manager who regurgitates all the ideas from your last email as if he thought of them on the spot? I find this quote a comfort in these situations. Unless it's a Zoom meeting. Then I find comfort in the 'mute' button.

In my early days in corporate sales, I recall being part of a brand-new team, a new division with new products, and a new manager. We were all sitting around the large meeting table, trying to outspeak each other, hoping to impress our new peers and our new boss. At one point, our manager asked, "Who wants to be the #1 rep on the team?" Everyone raised their hand, except for the quiet guy at the end of the table. Everyone's attention turned to him. He explained that his goal was not to be #1 but to do the best job he was hired to do. A year later, this guy was #1 not only on our team but in the whole country, and consistently retained that rank for years. He taught me a lesson: less talking and more doing, especially in our careers and business.

*Change is never painful; only the resistance to change is painful.*

–Gautama, The Lord Buddha

Sometimes people are difficult because they're having trouble accepting change. Like when a baby cries after the first time she sees her father without his glasses. It's a normal response to a break in their constant routine, and it's something to keep in mind when dealing with those for whom we are struggling to find empathy. Maybe we can ease their pain, or maybe they just need a nap.

*Walk away from anything or anyone who takes away from your joy. Life is too short to put up with fools.*

–Unknown

Realizing you need to walk away is one thing; doing it is another, especially if it's a close relationship. This quote is super helpful in making it happen. While it's fine to be in a relationship where once in a while the person we love influences our joy negatively, it's not okay if that becomes a permanent state. I use that as my guideline. What is yours? There are so many unchangeable circumstances that cause us stress in life, what's the point of holding on to the changeable ones? It's not only old clothes and boxes of books that "spark joy" but people too. Get rid of the ones who don't. (Thanks, Marie Kondo.)

*It is the mark of an educated mind to be able to entertain a thought without accepting it.*

–Aristotle

I find this helpful when trying to stay open to understanding others' points of view, but not necessarily making it my own. Learning the reasons why someone feels a certain way toward a matter is actually a great way to reevaluate your own reasons and make sure they truly match how you feel. It also makes you more agreeable and accepting. Or it makes you realize that certain people really are out of their minds. And if you find it worth keeping the peace, such as that difficult coworker or family member, sometimes you just need to agree to disagree. It's amazing the effect that concept can have.

*Whoever gossips to you, will gossip about you.*

–Spanish Proverb

This couldn't be truer. And I put it here in the "difficult people" category because, as sweet as some gossipers can be, gossip is corrosive to the trust aspect of any relationship. Some people use gossip as a way to disarm you while they are secretly filing away your opinions to share with someone else. This quote has helped me put that in perspective.

We have to watch out for these people everywhere in our lives, within our circles, at work, and in our careers. Avoid them like the plague. And if you can't avoid them, keep the conversation very shallow and never share anything personal with gossipers. You'll be no exception from their craft. And it's no use crying over spilt 'tea.'

*Endurance is patience concentrated.*

–Thomas Carlyle

God knows how much this is true, especially of those we find difficult to deal with. Life tests us once in a while by putting in front of us people who test our endurance. Let's hope that difficult person you have to endure is one who won't stay long, such as a customer in a store. But if it's someone constantly in your circle, it's time to rethink things. Is it a manager? A coworker? A loved one? Those are tougher to endure constantly, and, as a result, it means tougher choices. In the end, though, you are worth it. Being constantly stressed-out is not conducive to healthy outcomes in the long run.

Having the patience to endure rude individuals on a daily basis should be considered an Olympic sport. If you're in a work situation where you have to endure peers, or customers, who seem to have spooned an extra dose of 'disagreeable' into their coffee, make sure to take a shot of this quote with your breakfast. It may just help your concentrated patience.

*I can calculate the motion of heavenly bodies, but not the madness of people.*

–Sir Isaac Newton

Want to know the next time we'll see Hailey's Comet? No problem. Want to know about the orbital period of Venus? I'll tell you. Want to know why that woman in front of you is berating the teenage grocery clerk like it's their fault her coupon is expired? Sorry, can't help you out with that one.

There's no doubt that madness is like a virus in your computer. There's no pattern, nor is there any predictability, except for one thing: It's hazardous to all those around. It can incite mobs, destroy nations, and make it difficult to sit around the table together during holiday dinners. So, it's not worth arguing with those who don't make sense. Don't waste your energy and your brainpower. Their madness could be contagious! In these situations remember to just agree to disagree, and part ways in a healthy manner.

*If you wish to win a man over to your ideas, first make him your friend.*

–Abraham Lincoln

I know that sounds like an outrageous idea but given that we are all human beings with many things in common, we can start there as a basis for friendship. I'm sure that if we take the time to examine it, there are many more things that unite us than what divides us. And let's be honest, we are all more likely to hear someone out if we have an amicable relationship with them.

I love my politically opposite neighbors; we share bottles of wine and talk about many other things we have in common, such as golf, technology, real estate, food, travel. It is possible! Have we won each other over to our politically opposite beliefs and ideas? Probably not. But we treat each other with much care and respect and even tease each other come election day. That alone makes us see each other not as "the other" but as acquaintances. And that's a good start.

*Morality is simply the attitude we adopt toward people whom we personally dislike.*

–Oscar Wilde

How many times have I seen people pass judgment on people they personally have no connection to, yet if a close member of their inner circle does the same behavior, they excuse them away? It's such a human weakness! Why is it in this section? Because sometimes, we are the ones passing judgment on those we don't know, especially if we deem them difficult. How many times have we fallen for that morally grey character we hated in a book or movie after their tragic backstory was revealed? It can happen in real life too!

Once we get closer to that someone, our outlook changes. Mr. Wilde made us very aware of that weakness. He's right! Of course, it could also mean that we're the ones getting judged, but at least we're aware now and can do something about it. So sometimes you have to ask yourself, "Am I being the difficult person?" Because sometimes the answer is yes.

# NOTES

_____

_____

_____

_____

_____

_____

_____

_____

_____

_____

_____

_____

_____

_____

_____

_____

_____

_____

_____

_____

_____

_____

# Section 2:

## Our Relationship With Ourselves

On to the longest—and often most difficult—relationship we will ever have: The one with ourselves. The way we feel about ourselves changes the way we see the world. We are more likely to take the negative things said about us to heart when we are feeling bad about ourselves. (Especially if we are the ones saying them.) But when we are feeling confident in ourselves, those things roll right off our backs and down into the dirt where they belong.

Like any relationship, the one with ourselves takes work. Taking care of yourself goes beyond eating healthy and working out; your emotional health deserves just as much attention as your physical health. The things we feed our bodies and minds have a huge impact on our well-being. The lies we tell ourselves start to sound a lot like facts if we hear them often enough. So, while there is nothing wrong with poking fun at yourself every once in a while, maybe it's time to dial back the self-deprecating jokes that are really just digs at who you are as a person. It's time to meet yourself halfway.

Self-care has become a hot buzz word in the last few years and with good reason: It's vital to our existence. The specifics of self-care may look different to each of us. You could see it as taking a bubble bath in a candle-lit room with your favorite serial killer podcast on in the background, whereas your neighbor might enjoy getting lost in the virtual world of Minecraft for hours on end. But the basics tend to apply to everyone: You need to do the things in life that make you feel good.

The quotes in this section seek to strengthen the most important relationship in our lives. Whether you are looking to improve yourself by letting go of your vices or by gaining control of your financial future, these quotes will guide you through the journey of taking the time to invest in yourself.

# On Self-Improvement

*Reading is to the mind, what exercise is to the body.*

–Joseph Addison

For those of us who don't have much leisure time, both reading and exercise can be a luxury. We should still strive to do it, though, or we'll be totally out of shape in no time. And while physically being out of shape affects our health, mentally being out of shape has just as much of an impact.

Reading stretches your imagination, flexes your empathy, and strengthens your intellectual well-being. It doesn't matter if what you're reading is an encyclopedia on quantum mechanics, or a spicy romance between a billionaire CEO and her feisty rival, which is only available on Kindle Unlimited. All that matters is that you are, in fact, reading. So go and get that washboard, rock-solid mind. You're doing it right now!

*We are shaped by our thoughts. We become what we think.*

–Gautama, The Lord Buddha

No doubt about it. Have any of you read about our powerful subconscious mind? Those of you who have, you know what I'm talking about. And those of you who have not, I highly encourage you to look it up. We truly are what we think, and so is our personal world. Our thoughts impact how we respond to the people we meet, the places we go, and the things that we do.

We attract all that with the power of our minds. Turns out, if I think nice things about myself rather than negative ones, I'll actually start to believe them. Who knew? So, let's make sure our thoughts are positive, which is why I'm sharing this lovely book with you. And I'm so grateful and honored that you have joined me here.

*The achievement of one goal should be the starting point of another.*

–Alexander Graham Bell

No doubt about it. By adding new goals to our milestones, our lives are filled with purpose, and we grow as human beings. Pushing yourself to reach farther, do better, and achieve more is the only way to keep yourself moving forward.

The journey of self-improvement is one without a destination. There is always something about yourself that you can work on to improve and become a better individual.

*The only person you are destined to become is the person you decide to be.*

–Ralph Waldo Emerson

This goes back to how we shape our mindset: It all starts there. When we visualize who we want to become, our own energy will find its way there, as long as we do the work and keep visualizing. It's incredible; the things you are able to manifest for yourself when you put your mind and actions to it.

It's like that part in a video game where you get to design every aspect of your character. You get to choose your hair color, your clothes, your career, and the place that you call home. You are the hands on your own controller. Just don't forget to press 'start'.

⬥⸻⬥

*Things may come to those who wait, but only the things left by those who hustle.*

–Abraham Lincoln

You know, I grew up thinking that good things come to those who wait, but after reading this nice little twist by Ole Abe, I realized we better hustle because everyone else out there is. So, no sitting at home waiting for things to come your way. Just visualizing your deepest desires isn't going to make the significant other of your dreams appear in your living room. You have to put in the work as well.

Part of working toward self-improvement is finding your self-motivation. And what better to motivate you than the idea that you get the first pick of your desires if you do? Go out there and get it! (Also, does this mean Abraham Lincoln is the culprit of inventing "hustle culture"?)

# On Food, Weight Management, and Other Vices

*For success, attitude is equally as important as ability.*

–Walter Scott

It's so hard to give up cheese, or ice cream, or pizza, or whatever else we love to eat, but once our mindset changes, it happens. I used to be a social smoker in the late nineties, enjoying a good Dunhill cigarette with a glass of wine and a steak. But in the early 2000s, when I was diagnosed with cancer, I stopped social smoking, cold turkey! It was harder to give up the steak, but eventually I did that too. An occasional glass of wine still happens, but it doesn't feel as enjoyable as before.

Once my attitude changed about my little vices, my body responded differently. You can train yourself to like something and retrain yourself to dislike something as long as you have the determination. I chose life over those little pleasures or vices, and I'm still here. So, it's paid off so far. Stop telling yourself you can't do it. If you want someone to tell you your limitations, you should ask strangers on the internet. They seem to know a lot.

*To know how to wait. It is the great secret of success.*

–Joseph De Maistre

Waiting—for this impatient author—is so very difficult. Knowing how to wait is truly a discipline I work at constantly. I don't always succeed at this waiting game when it comes to food enjoyment but wait I must. Especially when that pizza needs to be in the oven for 20 minutes, or the tamales for 30, or the restaurant needs to make my favorite paella before the delivery person can even leave for my door. It's like waiting for that Ali Express order to arrive all the way from China! All this waiting should qualify a person for sainthood.

And then comes the time when all that needs to wait because healthy eating is a priority. The body does thank you, though, so it is all worth it. Even when you're not seeing the progress you want in the amount of time you think you should take. It can make you want to give up because it feels like all that work was for nothing. Give it time. Things are happening. Just wait and see.

*Our bodies are our gardens—our wills are our gardeners.*

–William Shakespeare

Oh boy! I won't lie. My garden can get pretty overgrown, underwatered, and in need of some good soil at times. We've all been there when our proverbial gardeners seem to go on an extended vacation, especially during pandemic quarantines. (Did anyone else just fly past the "covid 15" and gain every pound of the "covid 19"? Ah, good times.)

However, it takes just one look in the mirror—or trying to get into those great pants you bought last year—and you're reminded that the gardener needs to get back to work ASAP. You and your gardener have to figure out a schedule that works for both of you because you've got to work to make it bloom.

———————————————————

*Knowing is not enough; we must apply. Willing is not enough; we must do.*

–Johann Wolfgang von Goethe

How many of us are practically experts in the right foods, the right exercises, and the right health practices yet do not possess the right discipline? Guilty as charged here. I have a bad habit of investing time in learning about the things I need to do rather than just doing them, which is why I keep this quote close to me as a constant reminder. I hope it helps you too.

———————————————————

*To keep the body in good health is a duty. Otherwise, we shall not be able to keep our mind strong and clear.*

–Gautama, The Lord Buddha

I might try to convince myself that pounding back two family-sized bags of Lindor truffles is a form of self-care, but I'm only kidding myself (and that guy at the convenience store who asked if I was having a party). We all have our vices but taking care of our bodies is just as important for mental health as it is for physical health. When we are focused on our goals, we are that much closer to achieving them. So maybe next time I'll just go with the regular-sized bags.

*The reason most people fail instead of succeed is they trade what they want most for what they want at the moment.*

–Napoleon

Guilty as charged. And this particular quote is one that I don't see enough of in front of me. What I want right now does not always match up with what I want in the future.

I wish I would put in the work to run that marathon I've always dreamt of running, rather than marathon-watch Chopped from my couch. And if I want a cup of frozen yogurt at 9 p.m., I try not to think about my waistline or fitting into that favorite outfit I bought last year as I go to the fridge to get it. Oh! To be human! Guilty as charged, Mr. Napoleon. But keep trying we must.

*For a man to conquer himself is the first and noblest of all victories.*

–Plato

I have a friend whom I admire for her self-discipline, which no doubt has helped her achieve a lot, especially keeping a fine figure, from her time as a model in college and all through motherhood, to this day. She introduced me to the concept of checks and balances (which is dissimilar to what they teach you in eighth-grade government class).

She said if you go overboard on something today, make sure you make up for it the next day by eating lighter, or doing a detox. Just don't make it a habit of going overboard day after day, or it'll be that much harder to get back in shape. So, the times I've gone overboard, I would always remind myself of my friend's "checks and balances" concept. Though I don't have the figure of a model like she does, it's a solid reminder, and it has kept me from going past the point of no return, when it comes to weight control.

# On the Relationship With Ourselves

*You, yourself, as much as anybody in the entire universe, deserve your love and affection.*

–Gautama, The Lord Buddha

I'm one of those kids that grew up having to prove myself in order to feel lovable and accepted. Millions of us are, especially from prior generations. But the kids of the newer generations don't have it much easier, for now they have to deal with the disastrous effects of comparing themselves to photoshopped lives on social media. Self- love is an easy concept to grasp but a difficult one to put into practice.

So, this tenet about deserving love is something I've had to learn as an adult. It didn't feel true at first but, after much time, I've learned to practice it. What about you? There is nothing selfish about taking the time to appreciate yourself and the things you do. Being proud of your accomplishments doesn't take anything away from anyone else's. Don't be afraid to wine and dine yourself.

*Be yourself. Everyone else is already taken.*

–Oscar Wilde

Oscar Wilde, in my opinion, is one of the wittiest and wisest observers of human behavior, and this epigram is one of my favorites. There is something so freeing in realizing that it's okay, encouraged even, to just be yourself and everything that entails. Let's just keep in mind to offer the world the best version of ourselves, because that is how we'll be remembered. After all, look at the great names in history. You could be the next one.

*It is better to be alone than in bad company.*

–George Washington

Becoming my own best friend made me appreciate and discern the good versus the bad company. Once I got to know, accept, and like myself (this part is important), there were lines drawn that toxic people could not cross. Setting boundaries for yourself and the people you interact with, and holding firm to them, is the ultimate form of self-care. It took a long time to learn this, but I believe in this tenet, and it has kept me emotionally healthy. Going for a drive, or to the movies on my own, is as natural as going out with friends. It's an emotional independence that feels good to have. Besides, who doesn't like a little me-time?

*The things that we love tell us what we are.*

−St. Thomas Aquinas

Based on this tenet, I'm an ice cream, cheese, and latte-loving, musical energy roaming through the world. Haha... I love how music and driving can transport you into a different mindset, freeing you from hurt or anger or sadness, at least for a moment. What about you? How would the things you love describe you?

---

*To love oneself is the beginning of a life-long romance.*

−Oscar Wilde

My dear Oscar Wilde was right. Once you discover you're a pretty cool human being who enjoys their own company, you can pretty much guarantee it'll last as long as you live. It's getting to that point that requires a substantial amount of work, but all you have to do is start. So, star in an enemies-to-lovers romance with yourself. Start by appreciating how adorable your quirks are, your compassion, your intelligence, your determination. Take a good look and realize how lucky you are to have yourself.

---

# On Money and the Financial Future

*You cannot escape the responsibility of tomorrow by evading it today.*

–Abraham Lincoln

I t's by paying our bills on time that we achieve financial freedom. Procrastination is a forbidden word when it comes to keeping our finances in order because putting them off will only double our stress. While it's tempting to spend that paycheck destined for the cable or cell phone bill on that new pair of jeans (on sale, today only!), tomorrow will be here, and so will the consequences. Crazy how that works.

*Success is not something to wait for, it is something to work for.*

–Henry Wadsworth Longfellow

Financial success is only something that we can achieve for ourselves. Unless we're trust fund babies, every one of us has to learn to manage our finances and make the best of it in order to achieve our financial goals. Not to mention there is something so satisfying in knowing that you are the reason for your success with money.

So, waiting for a bonus paycheck to arrive—or to win the lottery, or for that rich aunt to die and leave you something—is not exactly a smart plan for financial success. It's all about taking our financial destiny and driving it ourselves.

*By failing to prepare, you're prepared to fail.*

–Benjamin Franklin

And that takes us to the planning stage. Do you like Excel? You better start. Begin working on your budget spreadsheet and plan out your finances. You'll feel in control by planning for contingencies—and even the fun stuff in life—without stressing yourself.

No need to wonder how you will afford that next vacation you agreed to go on with your friends. With a solid plan for how to manage your money, you'll always be prepared. It never hurts to have a plan A, a plan B, and even a plan C. A good spreadsheet can help you keep track of those scenarios. It beats pencil and paper. You don't have to be an expert; with the basics, you can do it, and it's totally worth it.

*The reason most people fail instead of succeed is they trade what they want most for what they want at the moment.*

–Napoleon

You've seen this lovely little tenet in the section on food, weight management, and other vices, but it's here again because it's very applicable to our finances as well. How many times have you spent some money on going out for drinks with your friends, right after you decided you were going to buy some shares of that new tech stock you read about? Or when you borrow money from your savings account, promising yourself you'll put it back with the next paycheck but never do? In my younger days, I would do things like that. But once I learned my way around spreadsheets, all that changed.

There's something about putting your numbers in a spreadsheet, seeing it in black and white (or colors if you choose) that makes you more disciplined and able to think beyond the now. Try it if you haven't, even if you think you're allergic to spreadsheets. They used to make me break out in hives. Now though, I don't make financial decisions without checking it first. It's become my personal accountant. I feel in control of my finances. And it's free.

*He who has a 'why' to live for can bear almost any 'how'.*

–Friedrich Nietzsche

This goes back to the whole idea of discipline and keeping your eye on your own North Star. What's yours? Or who's your North Star?

Could be your kids, parents, your pet goldfish named Spaghetti, or even yourself. My mom has been the living example of this quote. She worked endlessly, sacrificed her time, and at times sleep, to ensure my brother and I went to good schools and had a promising future. Whenever I see this quote, I am reminded of her. And I'm sure many of you out there are doing the same thing and living by this same tenet, led by your own North Star. Whoever or whatever you choose to be your guiding light, allow them to lead you out of the darkness. You might spend a night or two where dinner is an apple and a cup of tea, but if you know what you're doing and why you're doing it, you'll get there eventually. I salute you all, my driven friends.

**Responsibility is the price of freedom.**

–Elbert Hubbard

Ah, yes, here's the word 'responsibility' again, but when it comes to finances, it couldn't be truer. The more financially responsible that commercial institutions (and nowadays future employers) perceive you to be, the more freedoms you're granted. Freedoms such as choosing a new car of your liking right out of the dealership showroom, or getting that cool apartment in a prime spot downtown, make the boring and dreaded term 'responsibility' a worthwhile endeavor. You'll be able to buy the newest toys, get prime interest rates, and even inch your way into that great job over the competition.

The key is making sure you can pay on time, or all those

freedoms get taken away. I do wish that schools had required courses in financial education, where students could learn what exactly is a 401k plan, how credit and investing work, what's compound interest and how it can work against you, or for you, so you're in great financial shape by the time you're ready to buy that house or car. Some of us are fortunate enough to learn early, and some of us have had to learn the hard way, but I believe it should be required teaching in all schools. With great freedom comes great responsibility, Spider-Man.

*The happiest people don't necessarily have the best of everything, they just make the best out of everything that comes their way.*

–Unknown

Those of us who were not born rich have learned to select where we can save our dollars, and where we must pay well in order to get the best. And you know what? Not everything we own has to be the most expensive brand. I buy my paper towels at Walmart, their store brand, and they do as great a job as the top name. But when it comes to fragrances, I go to Bloomingdale's. I save in one in order to afford the other, and I'm happy with both. Find your halfway point when it comes to acquiring things.

Whatever life throws your way, look for the opportunity to use it to make your life better. You know what they say about lemons and lemonade. It's true. I'm not one to say that everything happens for a reason when life deals us the worst situations, but I have found that even in those dark times, opportunities are present.

What's more, we were all given one precious gift, whatever our condition is, or wherever it is we live on this planet, and that's 24 hours in our day. No one gets more. No one gets less. It's how we spend and enjoy those 24 hours that count. Find the 'happy' in the things you can.

# NOTES

# SECTION 3:

## MAKING THINGS WORK AT WORK

Whether you're starting your first day as an ice cream scooper at Baskin Robbins or your thirty-fourth year as the CFO at a Fortune 500 company, the key to being successful at your job is knowing how to conduct yourself at your place of work. Being proficient at each aspect of your job is only a part of what makes you a great worker; the rest is made up of your attitude, your outlook, and your interactions with the other people who work there.

The fastest way to earn the respect of your coworkers, clients, and employers is with a kind and confident attitude. People want to work with someone who knows what they're doing and isn't a jerk about it. In spite of what is pushed on us by movies and television, there is no need to adopt a hard, stone-cold personality in order to be successful. Being firm and sticking up for yourself doesn't require beating someone else down. And while you don't have to become best friends with everyone at your workplace, maintaining a friendly disposition will get you a lot farther than an unapproachable one.

The majority of your week is spent at your workplace, and it's vital that you create a work environment for yourself that is healthy and productive. You might find yourself at a job that you don't plan to be at for long, or you might already have the career of your dreams. Either way, you should treat each employment opportunity as a serious chance to prove yourself as an asset to your company. View it as a way to develop your skills and determine what it is you truly want to do. And if that turns out to be your current job, fantastic! If you learn that you never want to work in that industry again, even better! Discover the things that will make you happy to go to work every day.

Each quote in this section helped me to "make things work at work." Regardless of what is outlined in our job description, we have the ability to be a leader amongst those we work with, and I'm sharing them with you to help you achieve that and more. There are helpful sayings for every type of relationship you will encounter throughout your career, as well as advice on how to go about starting a new project. And for those times you may need an extra boost of encouragement and support when you are prepping for a big interview or presentation, there are quotes for that as well. Conquer that work-related stress like a boss!

# On Being a Leader

*A superior man is modest in his speech but exceeds in his actions.*

–Confucius

There is nothing poorer than a leader who, instead of speaking in terms of 'we', talks about the 'I' and 'my' and how wonderful they are at doing things—especially if their actions do not match their words. These are the people who view their leadership position as an excuse to conflate their power with their self- importance. They spend so much time thinking they are the hero that they end up acting like the villain. It clouds their ability to actually lead and destroys their team's trust in them. Be wary of becoming (or working under) someone who spins tales of their work ethic and puts in more hours playing the back nine than they do behind their desk.

*If your actions inspire others to dream more, learn more, do more, and become more, you are a leader.*

–John Quincy Adams

Ah! That's the mark of a true leader, someone who brings out the best in us, who inspires us to be better and do better as a group. If you aspire to be a leader amongst your team, you need to look toward the people in your life who have motivated you, for example. Those are the people who show they care, who show empathy, who bring out our trust in them, their word, and their vision. Because that vision, we know in our hearts, has the best of intentions for the overall good, even if they make mistakes along the way. When life is a Game of Thrones, be a Jon Snow.

*You can easily judge the character of a man by how he treats those who can do nothing for him.*

–Johann Wolfgang von Goethe

We've all come across one of these people at some point in our lives, and we just know right away. They reek of smugness, narcissism, and too much cologne of self-importance. The question is, are we going to be that kind of leader?

More importantly, by treating everyone kindly, even if they can do nothing for us today, not only will it ensure good karma, but who knows? I am a firm believer that everyone in this world, no matter their background or status, has something to offer. The recipient of that kind of treatment may make it big one day, remember that kind moment when they had little to offer, and pay it forward. A beautiful cycle of appreciation (and maybe a brownie point or two).

*A great man is hard on himself. A small man is hard on others.*

–Confucius

How many of us have suffered under these demanding, uncaring leaders and managers at work? We all have our share of horror stories. Those people claim they're being hard on us because they want to make us better, but then we catch them going easy on themselves or breaking the rules to fit their needs. For example, that employer who berates you for being five minutes late just after they strolled in from their good three-hour lunch.

Whenever I've been through those experiences, as traumatic as they've been sometimes, I take comfort in knowing that such a person taught me how not to act. I don't ever want to be that kind of small little leader or manager. They are rarely remembered as someone who inspired—unless you count inspiring a full-on revolt. What kind of leader will you be?

*Nearly all men can stand adversity, but if you want to test a man's character, give him power.*

–Robert G. Ingersoll

Power corrupts. And too many people have been assigned to positions of power, where they proved not to have the chops for leadership by succumbing to the temptation that power brings. You have to keep a hold on all of the qualities that led to you obtaining that position in order to deserve it. If you start feeling the urge to growl "My precious!" while lovingly stroking your name plate, it may be time to step down.

*Love all, trust a few, do wrong to none.*

–William Shakespeare

And bring donuts for everyone. There are times when being selective is the way to go, but that is not the case when it comes to treating people with respect and compassion. Regardless of personal differences or disagreeable attitudes, everyone is entitled to be treated fairly by the one leading them. Every person who inherits responsibility for a team would do well to live by this Shakespearean tenet. They would get a good night's sleep, and so would the people working for them. (But seriously, don't forget the donuts.)

*The only thing necessary for the triumph of evil is for good men to do nothing.*

–Edmund Burke

A famous saying and so, so applicable to this day and age. God bless those who see an injustice and get up to do something about it. Too many of us choose to look the other way but, thanks to those who choose to do more, our society has a chance. It's up to you to decide if you are going to be the sort of leader who makes way for evil to win, even if it's inconvenient for you, or the sort who defeats it. Stand up for others, stand up for yourself, and stand up for when it's your turn to do the wave.

---

*Knowing what's right doesn't mean much unless you do what's right.*

–Theodore Roosevelt

As leaders, we're given leverage to make big decisions, the kind of decisions that affect many people, which is why it's not only important to know what's right but to also choose what's right. Too often it is easier to go with the path of least resistance, where it might be the best choice for you but not for the greater good.

There will always be other factors tempting you to take the easy way out, but in the end, can you live with yourself and the decisions you make? They may even come back to haunt you. So it's better just to do the right thing. Your conscience will let you sleep at night—and so will that monster living under your bed.

———————————————————————

*You can lead a horse to water, but you can't make him drink.*

–Old English Homilies, 1175

Ah! This is one of my favorite quotes ever! Sometimes we're not necessarily in a leadership position. At times we simply have the knowledge to help someone out of trouble, or guide them to a better situation, and we do it. But it can be so frustrating when despite our well- meaning efforts, they refuse to help themselves. Like when you set up the perfect opportunity for them to achieve their goals and they choose to do something else.

This is where this tenet comes in very handy to help you let go of the frustration. It's helped me take a step back and say, "Well, I brought the horse to the water." You did your part, now it's up to them to drink it. And unfortunately, there are times when they don't, so they end up still suffering despite your guidance. But at least you know you did everything you could. (Some stallions just can't be wrangled.)

———————————————————————

*Give a man a fish, and you feed him for a day. Teach a man to fish, and you feed him for a lifetime.*

–Maimonides

Last but not least, the best leaders, managers, parents—really anyone in a position of authority—empower others to achieve their potential. As a technophile and all-around techie, I have learned that as I help someone with their tech question, I make sure to show them how I solve it. That way, if they get into the same problem again, they know how to get out of it without needing my help. That means more time for me and a happy and technologically self-sufficient friend. What a satisfactory feeling it is!

Being the reason someone acquires the skills to create their own success will not only feel good but will also allow you to delegate, increasing the productivity of you and your team. After all, creating dependency on the people in your life, or your team, can increase undue stress for you and leave less time for you to do your things. Not to mention that your team will find learning how to do something for themselves is a huge confidence booster, even if it's a task they're not fond of. In this world, it's go fish or go home.

# On Career Relationships: Clients, Coworkers, Managers

*As I grow older, I pay less attention to what men say. I just watch what they do.*

–Andrew Carnegie

It is best to be observant, especially at work where your financial future is ultimately defined. You never know what you are going to see when you take the time to look around the workplace. It'll tell you a lot about the people around you. Who to trust, who to avoid, who keeps the best desk snacks for when it's four o'clock and you're starving; the essentials.

*Be less curious about people and more curious about ideas.*

–Marie Curie

This is the smartest approach at the workplace. The easiest way to sabotage your work relationships is if you are worrying too much about how other people are getting on with their jobs. If you focus on how fast Lisa completes an order or how many clients Mark now has, you'll start to feel unhealthily competitive.

This is not a time to compare and contrast with anyone but yourself. Mind your business and see how you can contribute to the business. The only person you should be curious about is the one in your mirror.

*Change is never painful; only the resistance to change is painful.*

–Gautama, The Lord Buddha

Another of those few quotes that you will see taking a different message in a new section. Now we are looking at it from the perspective of you feeling the pain of an unwanted change. How many times have we encountered change at work, whether it be from bosses, companies, takeovers, or new management? And how many times did we just absolutely abhor that change? Like socks with sandals, resistance is not a good look. Change is one of the constants of life: Be like water and flow easily into that new mold, not a block of ice that needs to be broken to fit in.

*A kiss may ruin a human life.*

–Oscar Wilde

So don't do it! There are always consequences when pursuing romantic entanglements at your place of work, and the majority of the time they fall into the negative category. No matter how tempting it is or how much fun it looks in all those workplace romcoms. I blame Hugh Grant. (Exceptions can be made if they are already your spouse or significant other. Then go ahead and kiss away!)

*We secure our friends not by accepting favors but by doing favors.*

–Thucydides

I'd say small favors that won't require sacrifice from us. Let someone borrow your office for a quick meeting or show them the best break room to heat their lunch in (not the one on the third floor). The right people in business will appreciate it and become friends. And if some people let us down, we won't lose much.

In life overall, however, I believe in doing favors but not expecting anything in return from the recipient. Usually, life takes care of returning the favor to us from someone else down the road. Hopefully in the form of an all-expense-paid trip to Europe or a delicious, sweet treat from that one bakery. I'm not picky.

*Do not repeat anything you will not sign your name to.*

-Unknown

This couldn't be truer at the workplace and throughout our careers, whether it's with co-workers or clients. Making a promise you know you can't keep, or sharing information that you aren't completely sure is correct, will be a fast way to secure mistrust. It'll keep us out of sticky situations and true to ourselves. Know what you're talking about, double-check your facts, and when in doubt, Google it.

---

*It is better to keep your mouth closed and let people think you are a fool than to open it and remove all doubt.*

-Mark Twain

An important quote to remember at company meetings. Being choosy with the comments you make will ensure they have a stronger impact, instead of saying whatever first comes to mind. I wish I had seen it during my younger days in corporate America. But I guess we've all been guilty of being "the talker" at the company meeting, especially if you're a member of the sales team where everyone is trying to outshine each other.

As I learned later, it's better to observe than try to show off to corporate in hopes of impressing them. Half the time, they're playing

Candy Crush on their phones under the table anyway. In the end, I learned it is your numbers, and getting results, that best do the talking.

*Don't give others what they don't want.*

–Japanese Proverb

Amen to that. It is right up there with that golden rule we learn in kindergarten about treating others the way they want to be treated. So, no betrayals, no gossiping, no taking advantage of those we work with. And no mugs. No one wants that many mugs. Instead, give them kindness. It always works.

*The best way to appreciate your job is to imagine yourself without one.*

–Oscar Wilde

There is no time like the present to be grateful for having a job, especially with the impact the pandemic has had on today's job market and unemployment rates. While it is easy to complain about our workplaces, we ought to think about the good in them. It'll keep our mindset positive and attract good things to our life and career. And, you know, make it so you are able to pay your bills, buy groceries, afford a trip to the ER when you slam your finger in the door because you were too busy complaining about work. The little things.

*The greatest discovery of any generation is that a human can alter his life by altering his attitude.*

–William James

Attitude is everything wherever we go, but especially at the workplace and throughout our careers. If you believe in yourself rather than doubt your abilities, you set yourself up for success. Employers are more likely to pick someone who is determined and easy to work with, over someone who might have a stronger skill set but a bad attitude.

And while we're talking about attitude, there is another aspect worthy of mention, and that is your actual attitude towards your leadership at work. Never, ever give attitude to anyone who has control over your schedule and your paycheck, regardless of your personal feelings. It could be an expensive proposition and one you won't win. So, play the game; develop an optimistic attitude at work. Avoid the naysayers—even if you agree with them—for it may cost you your success at the workplace. It'll make you stand out in the best way possible; like a unicorn in a herd of donkeys.

*Relationships are based on four principles: respect, understanding, acceptance, and appreciation.*

–Mahatma Gandhi

This I find to be one of the most important quotes anyone can keep by their side, which is why you see it mentioned again here in the career section. It is a very powerful one to live by and the basis of any successful relationship, whether it's at work or in your personal life. And successful relationships lead to success overall.

But let's say not all is sweet and dandy at work and you have a manager who does not observe these basic relationship concepts; maybe they treat you like a personal servant or like your work isn't as important as theirs. While it's human to expect good treatment from our bosses, once you recognize those who can't, try at first by treating them with these four principles. You never know, you may just 'Mr. Miyagi' them into learning something subconsciously, and they'll respond in kind. And if they are the sort who still don't appreciate it, try to find a way out of that relationship because it isn't healthy. No one deserves to be in a toxic relationship, especially with a manager at work.

*Responsibility is the price of freedom.*

–Elbert Hubbard

Just like financial responsibility is the price of financial freedom, responsible behavior at the workplace corresponds with professional freedom. Responsibility earns us the trust of our employers, and with time, it earns us freedoms and certain privileges, which lead to more responsibility. It's a wonderful cycle that often rewards us for doing the things we're supposed to do.

While some may view being responsible as boring—arriving early, staying late, covering a shift even when Netflix just dropped a new, binge-able series—it is the benefits of that responsible behavior that are exciting and will eventually put you in an enviable position.

*We have two ears and one mouth so that we can listen twice as much as we speak.*

–Epictetus

This is another key quote in the workplace. You saw it earlier in the section on close relationships, but I'd say it applies to all relationships, whether close, casual, or professional. At the workplace especially, it comes in super handy. It'll make us less obnoxious, more likeable, and it will provide us with valuable insight into how well we are performing in the eyes of our coworkers. Now, the main reason I have included it here as well is to address the importance of listening to our customers.

A customer, especially those repeat or long-term clients, deserves to be treated as such. Whether it's a customer buying a bottle of soda at the convenience store, or a major client purchasing a multi-million dollar contract, they'll continue to buy from you if they feel their needs and wants are heard and addressed by your products and services. So don't start by selling; start by listening. After all, we are all customers and can easily appreciate those businesses that treat us with respect, understand our plight, accept our shortcomings, and appreciate our business. Otherwise, we go elsewhere.

Of course, it would be nice if it's mutual, but that's not always the case in business. Customers can lie and may do all the talking with none of the listening. Yes, we've encountered those before, and you know they could use observing this quote. So, if it's one of those situations, let's hope the monetary reward is worth putting up with that type of customer. But from the business point of view, we must always apply this quote, regardless, to ensure loyalty, success, and in the time of social media, positive feedback.

*Man is the cruelest animal.*

–Friedrich Nietzche

When it comes to facing opponents, competitors, and sadly, enemies (let's hope you have none), this is something to keep in mind. If given the opportunity, the people who want to hurt you, will. They will look for your weak points and find a way to tear you down when you least expect it. So, keeping this quote in mind will help protect you as you face your competitors in life.

You're probably wondering why I would put such a negative view of humanity here. Well, as much as I'd like to tell you that everything will be kitten paws and puppy breath if you follow these quotes, there is always the need to be aware of the unavoidably ugly side of humanity. Having been in a very competitive field of sales and business development, I was witness to all sorts of selfish and cruel behavior— from fellow coworkers, competitors, and even clients and customers.

Not trying to put you off your Cocoa Puffs, I just want to acknowledge that while there are those of us who want to make the world a better place, there are also people walking among us who are only interested in making the world better only for themselves and screw the rest. So, be aware of these undesirable types of human beings and, hopefully, some of the quotes in this book will help you deal with them successfully, ensuring that you move past and over them. Besides, karma has the nose of a bloodhound and knows where to find them.

Ultimately, if you don't want to wait for karma, it doesn't hurt to read Sun Tzu's 'The Art of War.' This is another must-have book for any leader or strategic business person.

*I destroy my enemies when I make them my friends.*

–Abraham Lincoln

Can't stand that obnoxious coworker who always has to one-up you? Or that rep from the competition who never fails to get your blood boiling? It could be that you haven't done a thing to provoke their wrath, or it could be that they still hold a grudge from the time you unknowingly parked in their spot. What better way to beat them than to bring them around to see how awesome you are, turning them from foe to friend and, in some cases, to a fan.

As you may have noticed in this book of quotes, the prevailing message is kindness. Start with that: People tend to respond positively. And if you can't get through to them, you still get that delicious sensation of moral superiority for taking the high road. Trust me on this one; they will take note of your kind words and actions, even if they don't give you the reaction you expect. Human beings are funny that way. Kindness has a lovely effect. Plus, it's class at its best. It's one of the major lessons I've come to learn with time.

*A pound of pluck is worth a ton of luck.*

–James A. Garfield

In our careers, this quote couldn't be truer. We so often hear stories about a select few people miraculously getting a lucky break. Perhaps they knew someone in the business that they were trying to break into, they won a contest, or were randomly discovered on the streets of New York City. While we may be in awe of these stories, if we look deeper, these so-called 'lucky breaks' came to those who have been working and preparing for a long time, in anonymity.

Put in the work, get noticed, always be prepared, stand out from the crowd—in a positive way, of course!—and, sooner or later, you'll be considered 'lucky'. There's nothing like the sweet smell of totally earned success in the morning!

***

*Your own resolution to succeed is more important than any other.*

–Abraham Lincoln

No doubt about it. You can't rely on other people; for it is your belief in yourself that will make all the difference. Once we are resolved to succeed in whatever goal we put in front of us, our mindset will help us get there no matter the obstacle. You're making the choice, consciously and subconsciously, to do what needs to be done. I've found that as I work toward my goal, if I envision myself achieving it—allow myself to revel in the great feeling of getting there—my mindset becomes focused, and things begin to happen.

I remember interviewing for a job I really, really wanted. One that meant I'd be moving out of the admin pool and into an executive position at my Fortune 100 employer, where I would gain a ton of independence and new perks. It was a huge step in my career. As I prepared for my interviews, gathered reviews and recommendations,

I visualized myself driving home from a day already in that new position, watching the sunset, happy about a successful workday. Needless to say, I got the job, and it was a momentous step in my overall career. Never underestimate the power of manifestation.

*One of the first signs of a spirit-filled life is enthusiasm.*

–A. B. Simpson

Have you noticed how much more attractive and well-liked the people around you, who are generally enthusiastic, are? I call it the positive energy that attracts. People like to be around those who are genuinely enthusiastic about work, about life, about whatever they are into. There is nothing more enthralling than the unbridled passion of someone talking about their latest project. Be one of those, and you never know whose attention you'll pull your way. There is no better way to get noticed at the workplace than through a genuinely enthusiastic attitude.

Hopefully, your workplace is exciting to you, and if it isn't, find something that is. Not everyone is excited by spreadsheets and numbers; maybe you find excitement in those tiny, crocheted octopuses you sell on Etsy. Whatever it is you want to do, do it with enthusiasm.

*Luck is what happens when preparation meets opportunity.*

–Seneca

Last but not least in our careers, this is the one quote we must always remember. It is not only the undeniable truth, but it is the key to success. One thing I always recommend to anyone who is pursuing a career or a profession is to collect all the written kudos you get during your work life: personnel reviews, letters from managers, customers, your numbers, even newspaper clippings. Keep that in a handy file and create what those of us in the pharmaceuticals industry used to call, "The Brag Book." Photograph it, put it into sections, and walk into every job interview with that book in hand. Not only does it show you're prepared, but it's proof of the goods.

Nowadays, of course, LinkedIn is equivalent to that. I recommend always networking with people there and if you see fit, ask for a recommendation, especially from those in higher positions than you, or who've been your clients. I've heard of candidates walking into interviews where the managers have already made up their minds to hire them, solely because of the recommendations and kudos on their LinkedIn profile; they just want to meet them in person to seal the deal. That is the sign of someone who is always prepared with the goods for any opportunity that comes their way. So, brag-book or LinkedIn, or both. Even a billboard in Times Square if you've got the budget. Always be prepared for that next opportunity.

# Taking on Projects and Assignments

*The beginning is the most important part of the work.*

–Plato

It's like how breakfast is the most important meal of the day; how you set out to achieve something will determine how well it is going to go. Did I mention how important it is to volunteer to take on projects at the workplace during the course of your career? And if you did not volunteer but were assigned anyway, take it as a compliment and run with it. Special projects put you at an elevated status, especially if you are successful at it.

Why is this quote as basic as a latte art Instagram post? Because how you start is very telling of how successful you'll be at completing the project. Planning the project, for example, is key; it tests your managerial chops. As you know well, you cannot afford to fail in your planning stage. So, get to it. Your future awaits.

*Well done is better than well said.*

–Benjamin Franklin

Yes, do not be all talk and little action. In my years in corporate America I came across too many fast talkers who did as little as possible to contribute. It was frustrating to work alongside these time-suckers because not only did they fail to fully contribute, but too much time was devoted to making up for the parts they failed to accomplish. Avoid those people like you do a raccoon carcass in the middle of the road. And if they're on your project, make sure they are accountable to the whole team. Fast talkers and little doers are a detriment to any team. Out them diplomatically if they insist in their ways, for they could cost the success of your project and your team.

*Victory comes from finding opportunities in problems.*

–Sun Tzu

All projects are usually designed to solve a problem, but along the way they'll present additional challenges. Don't focus on how terrible the challenges are. This quote reminds us that, at times, opportunities present themselves as challenges, so view problems as such. You never know, it may lead to a new discovery. A perfect example was the successful failure that led to the discovery of the multi-million dollar blockbuster erectile-dysfunction pill. The scientists who were studying it—for control of blood pressure—

discovered that while the little pill failed to work as desired, it had an unexpected side effect that they were able to make into one of the most popular drugs ever. There is no doubt that their minds were open to other possibilities rather than focusing on what the little blue pill couldn't do. Keep your mind open for your own successful failures.

*Small opportunities are often the beginning of great enterprises.*

–Demosthenes

All great enterprises have had their modest beginnings, and in my opinion, all great stories usually have humble beginnings. At the workplace, sometimes a small project can be the start of a series of bigger ones coming your way—to your advantage—just because you outdid yourself on the first. So, look for those small opportunities: That website that you created to share pictures of your cat in tiny outfits might just be the next Wayfair.

# NOTES

_____

_____

_____

_____

_____

_____

_____

_____

_____

_____

_____

_____

_____

_____

_____

_____

_____

_____

_____

_____

_____

_____

# Section 4:

## Dealing With the World Around Us

Our will is tested at every turn by challenges that we see coming and by those we don't. Facing the unknown is a hard task for anyone, but especially those of us whose anxiety skyrockets when we don't know what to expect. Our minds try to prepare us for every possible scenario as we dwell on all the things that could go wrong. It's exhausting.

The news that trickles in from our televisions, phones, and talkative neighbors doesn't do much to help settle our nerves when the majority of it is coated in negativity. It can be incredibly difficult to manage the balance between staying informed and not drowning in an endless stream of unsettling updates. We do our best to walk that tightrope, but it is inevitable that we will tip to one side or the other as time stretches on.

It takes a lot of energy not to translate that fear and anxiety into wicked road rage. When someone is driving so close behind you that they are practically in your backseat—despite the fact that you are already going 10 miles over the speed limit—and you begin to slow down just to piss them off. Add in those times when your 30-minute commute turns into a 90-minute commute and it's a wonder that any of us still have our license.

The following section is composed of quotes that will help you take that deep breath and gather your wits before dealing with the world around you. Reading these in times of stress will help you center yourself. You'll find the motivation to tackle those challenges, manage your news in-take, and find peace while on four wheels. I wish I could promise you that you'll never face a difficult situation again, but I don't live in a magic lamp. What I can do, is share with you these valued mental markers that serve as my north star. They keep me focused regardless of what goes on in the world around me, and I hope they do the same for you.

# Dealing With Challenging Situations and the Unknown

*Fortune sides with him who dares.*

–Virgil

O r she, who dares. Going for that promotion that seems just out of reach? Or on that interview for the job you'd sell your left kidney for? How about giving a presentation that could earn you top-level money? Whatever you're preparing for, dare to do something different. How many stories exist out there of people who set out to do the things they were told they couldn't? Of those who dared to defy the odds? I wouldn't be surprised if you have your own story. Or perhaps you will soon. Life can be exciting that way. So, stay bold. Keep pushing those boundaries and making sure you do the work too (very important!). Chances are fortune could be on your side.

*It is not the strongest species that survive, nor the most intelligent, but the most responsive to change.*

–Charles Darwin

Facing a major challenge? Have the dynamics in your life changed in a way you're not happy about? Are you facing an upcoming event that'll prove to be difficult? Don't think about how terrible it'll be or how much you wish it were different. At least not for long. Instead, adapt. Visualize how you can adjust to those new circumstances. Mentally, you need to remain pliable.

When my cancer returned with a vengeance, five years after the original diagnosis, I was scared. I had let down my guard, relaxed my own rules of staying healthy, and I knew then that death was one of the options. So, in my notebook, I wrote down Option A, Option B, Option C, and Option D(eath). I knew I had to modify my behavior—and my mindset—to face this new challenge. In my case, it meant embracing chemo and radiation as a possibility to save my life, something I had previously rejected and dreaded. But I had to do what I had to do. And that was my option B. Thankfully, I didn't have to go beyond that. (Option A was returning to my original homeopath, who had previously treated my earlier form of cancer successfully—or so I thought.) No doubt, challenges move us to grow and change. Because if we don't, we may break.

*Remember that guy that gave up? Neither does anyone else.*

–Unknown

Don't be that guy, or gal. It won't feel good.

Recently I was reminded about this quote when someone in my family was in the process of deciding between changing cars or turning in her lease. She saw quite a few showroom sales reps from a few brands she was considering. The last rep told her it was best to keep her leased car and buy it. It was the sensible thing to do, but it was a car she wasn't crazy about. She had seen a new, higher-end vehicle earlier, one that she really wanted, but wasn't sure if it was a good enough deal. In the end, it was the guy who didn't give up on her, the one who tried to find out what it'd take for her to get into that new car, who ended up getting her business. He understood how much she really liked it and tried his best to help her afford it. Eventually, he offered her what he himself called "a stupid deal." It was the end of the month, he needed to make his numbers, and he was determined not to give up. Now he is remembered warmly by my family member for helping her get into the car of her dreams, she's even saved his name and number in her phone book. And she sends him potential customers every chance she gets. I couldn't help but be reminded of the importance of persistence— reasonable, caring, empathetic persistence—not the annoying telemarketer-type trying to reach you about your car's extended warranty.

*Men cease to think when they think they know it all.*

–Horace

You're wondering why I would put this little quote here, in the section on dealing with challenging situations and the unknown. It's simple: When we're facing difficulties and scary times, we're being pushed to be creative. We're forced to think of new ways to solve a problem and it opens our minds again, the way it was when we were young and the world was new to us.

At times, as we get older, we reach a point in our lives when we think we know quite a bit—deservingly so as we've lived, achieved, and learned enough—and we've settled in our ways of thinking. But it is the unknown, the fear of something unpleasant coming our way, that forces us to think and learn new ways to adapt. So, I believe sometimes life offers us these challenges and scary possibilities to dare us to think again, to change our ways and mindset in order to survive. Or we may not.

*It's just a bad day. Not a bad life.*

–Unknown

It's striking how often we need to be reminded of that. Having a terrible day? Maybe you pulled out of the gas station with your wallet on top of your car, and its contents were flung across the intersection. Then you went home to help your 13-year-old with their math homework, but it was all gibberish and you both started crying. Then you stepped on a Lego, again.

Keep this little quote in front of you, whether it is on your fridge door or your computer monitor. Better yet, put it in your calendar alerts for it to show up once a month, perhaps at the end of the month when you have the most pressure at work, or at home when it's time to pay bills. Have it set annually, or monthly, as a reminder that the good outweighs the bad.

There are times when reminders like this pop up in my calendar unexpectedly, but with perfect timing. Now, if you find yourself having too many bad days, too often and too consecutively, perhaps it is time to rethink your life. And that's where the Fortune Favors The Bold quote can come in handy.

*Succeed despite*_____ *(fill in the blank)*

–Maria C Vale

This is a saying that a fantastic teammate and I came up with after enduring a tough manager. He was well-meaning and usually fair, but being new at the job he was not flexible and expected perfection from his team. Whenever he came out on field rides with us, he would leave us exhausted, especially at the end of the day when his reviews were mostly negative. It was so demoralizing that the next day we had no energy or motivation to get back in the field to do our thing. Yet we knew that we needed to succeed, to succeed despite Frank's tough leadership style. So that became our inspirational motto. Succeed despite Frank. Succeed despite our competition. Succeed despite the high quotas. Succeed despite feeling tired, despite the snow, despite the car breaking down.

Within a year, we were in the top ranks of our team. And Frank himself promoted us! For every time we felt demoralized and let down, we'd tell ourselves, "succeed despite " (you fill in the blank). It's a motto that I've used to this day, and I'm so grateful it came out of a challenging situation. I invite you to make it part of your life. It inspires me during those tough times, and I hope it does the same for you.

*Knowing what's right doesn't mean much unless you do what's right.*

–Theodore Roosevelt

Yes, we saw this little quote appear in the leadership section, because it is key in leadership. But it is also key when facing challenging situations, or the unknown; because when we are unsure of the outcome, doing what's right is the one thing we can control and rely upon. If we know nothing else about the potential outcome of a situation, it is always best to do what's right. Of course, what makes these situations challenging at times is that they make it so much easier to do the wrong thing. We may not know what the outcome will be at the end of the challenge, but we can be certain that doing the right thing, in the end, is always a winning choice.

Many years ago, during my days as a young, green rep calling on doctors, I came across what we call in the industry "a big writer." These are doctors who are identified as being busy, seeing tons of patients, and writing tons of scripts out of their practice, usually in the drug specialty we're representing. Promoting my new allergy drug was proving difficult. My main competitor had been there at least a year before, and though their drug wasn't as effective, it had a slightly lower incidence of sleepiness. So, you can imagine how excited I was to see this big writer in my territory, who was writing tons of scripts for my new challenging drug.

When I went to visit him, I was so grateful. He told me he had found it to be super effective and was just telling his patients to take it at bedtime. But what he told me next felt like tiny, frozen mice running down my spine; if I wanted him to keep writing the same level of scripts for my drug, he was going to need a steady monthly check of an amount I won't disclose here. He told me he made the same proposition to my competitor, and they had accepted, so it was only fair that I knew what I was up against. My heart sank to my stomach. I sure wish at that moment I had had a recorder. It felt so wrong, so corrupt! I wanted to give him a piece of my mind and tell him what he could do with his offer. Remembering my personal rules of conduct, though, I was diplomatic and told him I'd bring the offer to my District Manager.

My DM, the tough-but-fair guy, felt the same way I did. We looked at all the top writers in my territory and this crooked doctor was my highest. We decided to do the right thing and refuse his offer, take the hit, and make up the business elsewhere. And take the hit we did. The number of scripts for my drug out of his office dropped like a hot potato, and my competitors' went to the top, but I did manage to make it up elsewhere, while still diplomatically seeing this crooked doctor. A year later, I ran into my competitor coming out of his office. She looked upset and told me that this doctor was never happy, that no matter how much they did for him, he always wanted more. Being my competitor, that's all she said. After all, despite our feelings as competitors, we were on friendly terms. But I knew what she was talking about. By then, I had found new ways to promote my drug with great success, and I was giving them a run for their money. Shortly after that encounter with her, to my shock, this doctor started writing my drug again without us having written a single check to his name. In the end, we did the difficult but right thing, and it turned out alright.

# Dealing With Constantly Negative
# News Streams

*The happiness of your life depends on the quality of your thoughts.*

–Marcus Aurelius

There's no doubt many of us dread turning on the news nowadays, but alas, we must stay informed. So, what to do when at the end of the news segment it feels like the world is going to hell and you're being dragged along with it? Yes, disconnecting is an option, but you don't want to be the bird with its head in the sand and come across as uninformed to your peers. Whatever your preference for news outlets and your way of processing the information, it isn't about the source; it's about how you take it and let it affect your mindset.

Yes, it's easy to get angry, to curse at the screen or whichever pundit is on. Actually, you know what, do that for a minute or two—it can be cathartic!—but soon after, how are you moving forward? The first question I often ask myself, when I hear something terrible happens is, how much control do I have over this situation right now? If the answer is none, then the next question is, what can I control now?

And this is where this little quote comes in handy. We can control the quality of our thoughts. Yes, it is only human to get frustrated and, in the right circumstances, that's a handy motivator to do something to change a situation we don't like. But when we have no control at the moment, we turn to the things we can control, and that's the quality of our thoughts. After playing fantastic scenarios in your mind about how to change that undesirable situation that you really can't, begin to visualize a situation that makes you happy, something that is within your reach, such as going on a romantic getaway with your mate, or buying that house of your dreams with the boat dock in the back. So, forget about situations you can't control now, and focus on what you can. And give it tons of positive thoughts. (Go ahead, go crazy playing fantastic scenarios in that case!)

You want to visualize world events coming to fruition to your liking? Sure! Why not give it a shot? Just don't be disappointed if it doesn't work, for those things are way outside your control, unless of course, you are the President of the United States (and even that poor soul cannot control everything, no matter how powerful they are perceived to be).

*We're all in the gutter, but some of us are looking at the stars.*

–Oscar Wilde

This is another of my favorites. As you may have noticed, I'm a fan of Oscar Wilde. He wasn't only right, but his wit was priceless and, for the most part, he tends to hit the nail right on the head with his famous epigrams. This one is inspirational, and I put it in this section because, like in the prior quote, things may be what they may be, but we need to keep our outlook upwards. In my opinion, that means not only thinking of happy, desirable outcomes, but visualizing them, feeling them, and being grateful for them.

It's what I call weird mental magic, but there is something metaphysical about the concept of quantum leap in our cells and all that (Ant-Man was onto something). It can help our subconscious mind lead us to our desired outcome, or at least the outcome we dedicate most of our thoughts to, so we better keep those thoughts positive. If we continually focus on looking downwards, we may be telling our subconscious minds to make those negative thoughts come true too.

*Without music, life would be a mistake.*

–Friedrich Nietzsche

Lastly, but not the least important, I want to share with you how I, like many of you, deal with the stressful stuff heard on the news. After listening to the morning updates, I turn to music. Music is so personal. It's like colors or perfume; it all depends on how it blends with us.

This is my theory: Just like food feeds the body and is savored through the mouth; music feeds the soul, the mind, and is savored through the ears. So, after hearing the crazy news cycle, do some good mental palate cleansing by turning on your favorite playlist. And don't just turn on one of those stations with commercials; they'll only serve as a distraction to your soothing thoughts and detract from whatever effect the music is having on you.

Also, a tip here: When doing some mental palate-cleansing, avoid music with lyrics. Nothing wrong with music with lyrics, but sometimes lyrics can prove to be a distraction or have a message that is incongruent with your thoughts at that moment. For mental de-stressing I recommend upbeat instrumental music, whether it's classical, jazz, electronica, or baroque; it's up to you. Personally, I prefer music with 120-130 beats per minute to keep me moving and cheery throughout the day. You don't want music that will relax you so much you'll be ready for a nap, or sad music that will bring you down. I find that electronica is a good medium genre, such as deep or tropical house. With its nice kicks, high hats, and melodic synths, it takes me to positive places and lets my mind do the happy thinking, but it's all a matter of personal preference. So, avoid lyrics, unless those lyrics help you, which some songs are gifted that way. But nothing of sadness, anger, or disappointment. Keep it positive.

There are plenty of studies about the positive effects of music on the brain. One article in the highly respected medical journal, The Lancet, talks about how music helped patients recover after surgical procedures and that some did not even need as much pain relief (Hole et al., 2015). So, if you have better outcomes after listening to music, from something as traumatic as a surgical procedure, how about applying it to the at- times-traumatic effect of the daily news cycle? It's what you can do at the moment. Of course, long term, perhaps you can do something to fix those problems around the world and, who knows? It may include participation in the ballot box.

# Staying Sane Behind the Wheel

*Peace comes from within, do not seek it without.*

−Gautama, The Lord Buddha

I love driving. Whenever I get a chance, I love to get behind the wheel. For the most part, I find the experience soothing, until I run into the craziness of other drivers on the road. Then my mental Zen comes apart, and the tough, impatient New York City driver wants to take over. But I also know that whatever those crazy drivers are doing, for one, it's outside my control, and two, for the most part, it isn't personal. Everyone is in their own world and wants what they want in their nice comfy bubble of metal and glass. So, while I realize that not everyone is going to drive to my liking— especially those who have yet to discover the function of their turn signal—how I feel about that comes from me.

Sure! Rudeness on the road is hard to accept; in fact, it infuriates me. And yes, at times we put our egos to the accelerator and press down hard, but that isn't always our wisest choice. And what does that do for our mental peace? Not much. For our personal satisfaction? Perhaps some. But is it worth the potential for escalation into an undesirable or uncontrollable situation? No. So, do your part on the road by doing the right thing and let the knuckleheads make fools out of themselves, by themselves. It takes practice and experience to be a smart, fast, cunning driver who, at the same time, is patient enough to maneuver the roads safely nowadays. Have a good, dependable dashcam for it'll give you peace of mind should anything unsavory happen.

Put on your favorite music and don't let the rude knuckleheads get to you. Okay, maybe for a minute or two, but then let it go and move on. One of the homeopaths I saw years ago told me that it was actually a good thing to curse (inside your car cabin, of course!). These days, with so many angry people on the road, and with gun laws being so loose, you're better off keeping those words inside your cabin.

As my homeopath said, let it out. Don't hold it inside of you, unless you have people in your car who'll be offended. In that case, if you have the gift of humor, say something funny about the situation, it'll dissipate the tension. But if you're on your own, go ahead and curse like a truck driver all you want, just be sure to drive with class. That's how I keep my mental peace and sanity behind the wheel. It's all up to us.

*It is not the strongest species that survive, nor the most intelligent, but the most responsive to change.*

–Charles Darwin

Oh! The Darwinian mindset is the only way to survive on the road and avoid sticky situations. With so many bodies trapped inside metal boxes torpedoing down the road at different speeds and in all different directions, the only way to stay safe is to be constantly alert and flexible to change. Have a crazy speed demon coming up behind you on the right, swerving lanes like there is a swarm of bees controlling the wheel? Stay in your lane at your current speed and let them pass you. It's never a good idea to try to cut them off or engage them in a race. I laugh sometimes when that happens, because it tends to influence the other drivers around me. As soon as the speed demon passes, I see several cars try to follow suit. That certainly prompts an eye roll from me. Seriously people? But to each their own.

With the rapidly shifting environment of the roads and highways, we can make it home safely at the end of the day by staying alert and adapting to those constantly changing circumstances. That means not taking our eyes off of the road. Yes, I'm going to get preachy here. That means no texting while driving, as that will disable your ability to respond to unexpected and sudden events. Do not put yourself at a disadvantage. I keep my phone in a holder in front of me and, as tempting as it is to open that possibly important text I just saw arrive, I tell myself that it can wait. Sometimes life or catastrophe boils down to a few seconds. Could you imagine if you got into an accident because of a text sent by Domino's for 20% off your next pepperoni pizza? Be a Darwinian success: Stay alert at all times so you can respond to the constantly changing environment of the road.

*Good judgment is the result of experience and experience the result of bad judgment.*

–Mark Twain

Oh! This quote makes me laugh every time. And I chose to put it in this section because, while it applies to just about every aspect of our lives, it couldn't be truer to our time behind the wheel. Now, on a quick aside, I will mention here that I understand the new generations are not keen on driving, and someone once said that the babies born this second decade of the 21st century will not be driving as adults, but there is something very freeing and satisfying about driving. So, if you're one of those shiny new humans born in the new century, who doesn't care about driving, I'd like to invite you to try it. Why rely on others, or technology, to take you places? Being able to drive yourself gives you control and independence. So, try it. You may just like it.

Bringing us back to this quote, experience—especially behind the wheel—will involve some early bad judgment, and there is no doubt that is what insurance companies are banking on. Chances are that as you begin to drive, you will get into an accident or two, where it could be your bad judgment or the other person's. But, bottom-line, understand that fender benders and other scary moments are a part of learning. As we acquire this experience, the way to keep those mishaps down to a minimum is by having a reliable dashcam, keeping your eyes on the road, and being ready to respond quickly to the changes ahead of you. It's like a video game, except that it has real-life consequences (so maybe don't apply those Grand Theft Auto skills here).

During my early years driving, from sixteen through my twenties, I had a total of five car accidents; among them, one was major and the others were minor. Only two were my fault. Those car accidents taught me that being alert, defaulting on the rules, and adapting to the changing road circumstances was key to staying alive and sane. I probably sound like the DMV manual, but only after those accidents, a few tickets, and a couple of court dates did I come to that conclusion. So, I'm passing that experience on to you so that you will keep your own road misfortunes down to a minimum.

*Common sense is not so common.*

–Voltaire

Oh my God! How much do we find ourselves agreeing with this quote? If we try to figure out why people do the things they do on the road, we'll have a higher chance of solving the Collatz Conjecture (which no mathematician can currently solve). We cannot apply logic to some of the knuckleheaded things people do on the road. So, keep your inner peace and let them be.

*For every minute you are angry, you lose sixty seconds of happiness.*

–Ralph Waldo Emerson

Now, this is a quote that I could use in front of me every time I'm on the road. I'm far, far from perfect, which is why I need these quotes as mental markers to keep me sane and thriving in spite of all the craziness surrounding us. And yes, my impatience can easily turn to anger. I work at this every day. I think at this point in my life, I've lost hours of happiness due to my anger (or, you know, a month or two).

But anger is normal, and I've come to accept that. Where I often succeed is in not staying angry, for that lingering anger can be corrosive. Again, I am reminded of what one of my old homeopaths said, "Let it out and move on." So I say let's be like champagne: Bubble up to the surface, cause the cork to pop, but in the end, remain elegantly alive and still, ready to celebrate the good things in life. Cheers!

***

*Better to lose one minute in your life, than your life in one minute.*

–Latin American Proverb

This is one proverb I heard over and over from my mom while growing up, first when crossing the streets in New York, and eventually when I started driving; and it would prompt an eye roll from me, every time. While it can easily apply to so many aspects of our lives, here is where I think it has the most value.

Do we wait that extra minute on that red light? Or do we go through the yellow (and almost red) to save ourselves the extra minute? Not long ago, I was in a rush somewhere, and as soon as the light turned green, I hit the accelerator hard. Out of the corner of my eye, I saw someone trying to catch the last of the yellow going into the intersection, right in my direction. I was lucky to react quickly enough to stop, but certainly that driver was in a bigger rush than I, and not willing to lose that minute on the red light. Perhaps his mom never shared this famous proverb with him.

# NOTES

# Section 5:

## Things Outside Our Control

Sometimes the unexpectedness of bad news can be just as painful as the news itself. As hard as we may try, predicting the future is outside our realm of capabilities. Losing a job, a beloved pet, or a close friend, hits us hard in ways that are difficult to prepare for, and can toss us into the deep end of depression. Once we get to that point, we often have trouble pulling ourselves out. The best thing we can do is strengthen our mental well-being before such things happen so that we are able to handle whatever life throws at us.

Receiving bad news is a lot like getting pooped on by a seagull while enjoying your beach vacation; it comes out of nowhere, unpleasant and ready to ruin your good time. Little things, like learning that your favorite sweater shrunk in the laundry or that your toddler threw your cell phone out the window on the freeway, can build upon each other until the stress of it all threatens to make us explode.

Then there is the loss of a loved one. Whether this is from a falling out or someone is taken from our lives too soon, it is a devastating occurrence. It's human to expect to always have those we love around us, and it's human to be heartbroken when we lose them. So, it's okay to be sad, to be angry when that expectation isn't fulfilled. Give yourself the time and space to feel the loss; but be prepared throughout life with the knowledge that at some point, we could lose people we love. It's so important that while we have them around, we show them the appreciation they deserve.

On top of everything, we have the possibility of heartbreak coming at us from all angles. Romantic, platonic, and familial relationships have equal opportunities to tear our hearts into confetti-sized pieces and shoot them out of one of those New Year's Eve poppers. We can't control what the other people in our lives do, we can only put our trust in them and hope that they have our best interests at heart. Trust is hard to earn and even harder to give, but it is the key to every relationship.

This section strives to equip you with quotes that will armor your mental health with the strength it needs to overcome the hardships that life sails into you. While we don't know when bad things might happen, we do know that they are always possible. And when they do, it is perfectly normal for you to grieve, to allow yourself to feel every emotion that they evoke from you. The struggle is fighting to come back from the depths of your feelings and finding the power within yourself to keep going. These quotes will help you get there.

# Dealing With Bad News and Losses

*It's not what happens to you, but how you react to it that matters.*

–Epictetus

I'm a control freak. So, when things outside my control happen, and they happen often, I try to focus on what I can manage. That is my attitude, my reaction to what's being thrown my way. Sure, it's easier said than done. Lost your job? That big client? Missed that promotion? Lost someone? Your team lost? Were you mugged? A married, upper echelon creep made an unwanted pass at you at work? All you want to do is scream, run away, and curl up under your sheets. I get it, it's the human thing to do. But in order to get past that reaction, you have to control it. Then let your head take over.

The mind is amazing when unpredictable things are coming your way; it's already computing the multiple options to manage a situation. Your mind should be in control, not your emotions; they're no help when encountering undesirable situations. Believe in yourself and your ability to overcome the situation, whatever it is.

*Positive anything is better than negative nothing.*

–Elbert Hubbard

There's something to be said about getting back on the horse as soon as possible, for I believe the longer we permit ourselves to dwell on our losses, our self-pity, our why-me, the harder it is to get back up. When in the midst of wallowing in our current misfortune, as we lick and heal our wounds, one sure way to get us started back on the road is to focus on what we still have, on what remains. Even if you feel 99% of your life is going wrong, there is still that 1% that is working out for you. Focus on that one single thing that's good and use it as your crutch to get mentally back up.

It could be something as simple as being able to walk out of the hospital on your own two feet, after a few weeks as an inpatient; or being happily greeted by your pet when you get home, or waking up to a new day when you can start over. Start there. Everything else will follow.

*The greatest test of courage on Earth is to bear defeat without losing heart.*

–Robert Green Ingersoll

There isn't a single person on this planet who hasn't experienced some sort of loss or rejection. No one. Not even that gorgeous model you saw on the L-Train, the person at work who seems like they've got it all together, or even Oprah. All of us have, at one point or another, encountered that sinking feeling of defeat in the face of something we desired. So, always know in your heart that defeat is a natural part of experiencing life. It is only a beginning, and it is up to you to define how it ends. Never let it keep you down.

In fact, remember that little segment we covered about anger? I find at times that anger toward ourselves for not getting what we want is an excellent motivator. It can energize us to figure out what went wrong, learn from that, and if possible, strive for that goal again until we get it. Remember the story of my days as a pharma rep, promoting my beloved allergy drug that had the slightly higher somnolence side effect? The first few months of that year were tough; the competition kicked my butt, month after month. Everywhere I went, the doctors brought up that minor side effect, and some major specialists even made it clear they wouldn't touch my drug.

I felt like a pariah every time I'd visit an allergist's office, especially if I saw my competition coming out as I walked in. They'd sneer at me, and I'd feel so tiny and vulnerable. The competition had solidified its hold in my territory, and I felt defeated. My numbers were shameful. Actually, all of us on the team were suffering. One day, one of my favorite allergists, who I'd begun to see as a friend, was honest with me and told me she wouldn't consider my drug as first-line. I took that comment personally, and I became angry with myself for thinking it would be easy to overcome the competition. I went home early that day, checked into the local racquetball club, and smashed that ball hard against the wall for a good hour, imagining it was my competition. That's how hard I took it.

But that night, and the days that followed, I researched every aspect of my drug, inside out, study after study, and found the many advantages it had over the competition. That's why they were so scared of my product. During my studies, I had the good fortune of meeting one of the researchers for my drug, who was local at one of the most respected hospitals in New York. I went to him and asked him to teach me all about my product. He believed in it, extolled its superior efficacy, and told me why he used it as first-line, especially in his asthma patients, and how he got around the very low incidence of somnolence simply by having them take it at night. Asthma in the New York City boroughs, sadly, runs rampant. He taught me why my product was better than my competition. Turns out that many of the allergists in my territory saw him as an authority. He had been their teacher. So I enlisted him as my mentor and guide, and within a year, I was kicking my competition's butt.

A year later, that nice allergist who I considered my friend told me how much my competitors hated me as I was taking over their market share, and she was even beginning to use my drug as first-line with her patients. Another of my big writers, who had become a friend, jokingly told me to never let my competition catch me in a dark alley. I became an authority in my team, on the drug, and I had the highest sales in the country. I turned the shame of defeat around by not allowing the helplessness I felt at first to keep me down. I harnessed that anger and frustration of losing and found a way to come back with a vengeance. Instead of sitting back and letting my competition win, I armed myself with the knowledge I needed, and with an awesome mentor by my side, I made a success out of that initial defeat. There is always a win to be found inside of a loss. It's up to you to discover it. No matter how you do it, it's okay to feel defeated, just don't stay down too long. It's natural to lose heart for a moment, but not for good.

*Hard times will always reveal true friends.*

–Anonymous

There is always that one friend that will be there when no one else is. Most of the time, people don't know what you're going through until you tell them. As much as we wish those close to us could magically read our minds to know what's bothering us, they can't. (Unless you're friends with Edward Cullen. In which case, you have even bigger problems.)

If you don't let your friends in, you will never give them the opportunity to be there for you. As easy as it is to close off and isolate ourselves when going through hard times, it is okay to let our friends in. In fact, that's when we really see who's true. As I look back, I feel lucky to count on the people who have been there for me during the toughest moments. And there is always that one who stands out.

She was there during one of my traffic ticket court dates to make sure I wouldn't get in trouble by opening my smart, young mouth to the judge. She was there when my car got towed, and I had no idea where it was. She was there when I was really sick, and I needed to get to the ER. She was there to help me pack during my last move. I can only hope that I will be able to provide that same support when she needs me to be there for her. Though I've realized in life that what you do for others often comes back to you through a different person. So, I can only do for others what she has done for me through the years. To this day, I remain grateful to that lovely friend. I feel privileged and lucky to count her among those special people in my life.

*What does not kill me makes me stronger.*

–Friedrich Nietzsche

The way I see it, if we're still walking this planet, despite all that has come our way, good or bad, it only means we're stronger than before. How many of us have lost loved ones, jobs, homes, important competitions, our good health, but are still here, to live another day and tell our story? Despite calling your teacher 'Mom' or waving back to someone who was actually waving at someone else, you've survived humiliating moments that you never thought you'd get over. And sometimes you even look back and laugh about them! (Except that one thing. We don't talk about that one, though.)

If you've overcome a lot of adversity, know in your heart that you're stronger for it. Not feeling too strong after so much adversity? Understandable. It's only human to feel so. But in reality, you've developed a strength in survival that you never thought you'd have. And you need to recognize that.

*Fall seven times. Stand up eight.*

–Japanese Proverb

I've loved this Japanese proverb from the first time I saw it. I immediately had to copy it down and add it to my yearly calendar reminders. It's certainly a good reminder that falling does not mean we have to stay down; life is not about that. Life is about testing ourselves, pushing ourselves to the limit, and finding new boundaries beyond the horizon. And yes, there are times when we will fall painfully on our faces, but we won't find success and happiness by staying down after falling. So, as soon as we can, we owe it to ourselves to get back up, no matter how many times we fall, for so much is awaiting us down the road.

A perfect example is that we may lose a job in our lives at one point or another. And perhaps we won't be ready to let go. And it'll hurt like hell. No doubt it is like losing a relationship, but even more scary because this lost relationship is tied to our paycheck and, as a result, to so much more. While it is a painful thing to experience, especially if we're not prepared, we cannot allow ourselves to wallow in that loss. We literally cannot afford to stay down in that situation. You might spend some time imagining the worst-case scenarios and dwelling in self-pity, but use those very scenarios to dust yourself off, get up, spiff up that resume, and go at it with a vengeance. During your job searching, interviewing, and networking, who knows? You may even land a better opportunity. But never let yourself stay down.

You owe it to yourself, and your loved ones who depend on you, to succeed. Sometimes when you unexpectedly lose a job you loved, the best revenge for that situation is to land an even better one. So, get back up after the self-pity party. Show the world what you're made of. And think to yourself the words of that beloved 90s hit song, Tubthumping (also known as "I Get Knocked Down"), from the English rock group Chumbawamba (1997). It's no doubt a rock and roll ode to resilience.

So, go look it up. Listen to it. It's so good! It would make a fantastic personal hymn, especially after a setback. It's great if you blast it in your speakers. Just don't scare the neighbors.

# On Losing a Loved One

*Try and fail, but don't fail to try.*

–John Quincy Adams

Sometimes we lose loved ones, not to death, but to life; when they walk away and leave our world to follow other paths that lead away from us. This quote is a reminder that when a relationship is breaking down, and you fear you may lose that loved one, you have to make a choice on whether to let it happen or not. If that is the opposite of what you want, you must do whatever you possibly can to save that relationship. And if you're not sure? Imagine yourself, your life, without that person in it. That is the determining factor. So, if the answer is to save the relationship, you must try in every way, even if you are not successful. If you are, then great, but if you are not, at least you will know in your heart you gave it all you could.

*At some point you have to realize that some people can stay in your heart, but not in your life.*

–Unknown

And there are those times when you realize you're in a relationship so toxic that you have to let it go despite your strong sentimental attachment. To arrive at that conclusion is a huge deal. After so much toxicity, sooner or later, we begin to recognize how unhealthy our current situation has become. If that is the case, don't ignore that inner voice. That is your inner best friend pulling for you, trying to save you from drowning in someone else's world before you lose yourself.

On a personal note, there is someone walking this planet with whom I once had an amazing connection. But while our relationship started wonderfully, as the months went by, I began to feel short-changed. I started listening to my little inner voice, who kept screaming at me that I was being taken advantage of by that amazing someone. During that realization is when I came across this enlightening quote, and I knew it was a sign. It gave me the strength to pull away; and as much as it hurt for both of us to let go, I felt an inner relief in the end. Like I had regained myself once I was free from this toxic relationship. Don't get me wrong, it was messy, and it hurt like hell for both of us, but my loyalty to my inner self won over, and that's a move I'll never regret. I realized this relationship will remain beautiful in my heart, but that wasn't how it was in real life. Life may be a circus, but you are the ringmaster. Not only do you get to decide who you share a tent with, but you also get to decide which clowns you let go of.

*Life is a balance of holding on and letting go.*

–Rumi

This is the quote that brings me comfort whenever I've lost some of my loved ones, in one way or another. Life is indeed a balance of holding on and letting go. When it comes to losing the ones we love, there are two things left for us to do: to hold on to the memories and to let the people go.

One of my dearest and closest friends died too young years ago. And I mourned her for months, for years, to be honest. She had been someone I completely trusted, who understood me like no other. To this day, I'll never understand why she is no longer walking this Earth. That special friendship changed me in so many ways, and losing it was not easy. I mourned her loss privately for a long time, until one day she appeared in a dream and begged me to let her go. I remember in my dream refusing her request at first, but soon realizing I could hold onto the memories. It was true, I needed to let her go. And while that might sound like a plot I stole from a Lifetime movie, it actually happened!

Decades later, I have come to terms with that great loss, but I'm still holding on to the memories and the good moments we had. I find special comfort in this quote as I had to learn to walk this Earth and find that balance without my beloved friend to turn to. Whether it was a funny line or lovely text, no matter where in the world we found each other, her presence was always there. She needed to move on, but what remained were our memories. It wasn't easy. I had no control over that loss, but that is life: trying to figure out that delicate balance between holding on and letting go.

# On Heartbreak

*The broken heart. You think you will die, but you keep living, day after day after terrible day.*

— Charles Dickens, Great Expectations

Heartbreak will inevitably happen in one way or another. It could be in 50 years when death steals our loved one or in 50 minutes when that girl from the sushi restaurant does. It's the law of life. Expect it and give yourself the time and space when it does. And when it's over, wear it like a badge of honor, for you're now a decorated soldier of love.

*There is always a risk in being alive, and if you are more alive, there is more risk.*

–Henrik Ibsen

And heartbreak is one of the biggest risks to feeling alive. Are you going through heartbreak? Allow yourself to feel all of it. It's part of living. Hey! I know. It hurts like hell. God knows I've been there plenty of times—more than I would care to acknowledge—but the alternative is to feel numb, which is even worse. With time, heartbreak heals, and you'll be ready to feel the greatness of love again. Remember the Japanese proverb, "Fall seven times, get up eight." Yes, it even applies here.

*If the first button of one's coat is wrongly buttoned, all the rest will be crooked.*

–Giordano Bruno

Sometimes when we've ignored those red flags from the start, they come back to wave in our face, and that is how we end up heartbroken. So, we owe it to ourselves to pay attention to those red flags. For the sake of romance, we tend to ignore them, but if we're true to ourselves eventually we will come to the realization that a red flag is a red flag. And if there are more down the road, they are massive warnings. So, pump those brakes. Yes, it's going to hurt to let go whenever you make that decision, but the later it is, I can guarantee you, the more it's going to hurt and the more you will lose. So, pay attention to the beginning of your next relationship. And to the buttons on your coat.

*One can never pay too high a price for any sensation.*

–Oscar Wilde

I recall, in the midst of heartbreak in my college years, taking consolation in this famous Oscar Wilde quote. Sometimes the most amazing romantic moments with someone are worth the heartbreak later. Like eating dessert on an already full stomach, it feels so good in the moment.

---

*The worst thing about having a romance is that it leaves one so unromantic.*

–Oscar Wilde

And yes, this, at times, will happen. How many times have you swore you'd never date again after a bad break-up? In this era of dating apps and Instagram stalking, it feels like everyone else's romance is shoved in your face almost as soon as it ends for you, which can leave you feeling decidedly unromantic, true, but let's not stay unromantic for the rest of our lives. Life is less tasty when we lose our appetite for romance, especially when the world is full of total 'snacks.'

---

*A kiss may ruin a human life.*

–Oscar Wilde

That's pretty much heartbreak in a nutshell. Need I say more? I am sure you have your own story on that thought and, no doubt, one you can't share easily in public. But I won't make you kiss and tell. I put this Oscar Wilde quote here because its concept is truly romantic; it tells us that at times, one special moment is worth the inevitable pain later.

*Friendship is certainly the finest balm for the pangs of disappointed love.*

–Jane Austen

And if we try and fail, there are always our friends, thank goodness. Leaning on those close to us for support, when our hearts have just been food-processed into hummus, reminds us that we still have love in our lives. Maybe not the romantic sort for the time being, but love nonetheless. It is a time when the importance of friendship is on full display, for they are indeed a fine balm for heartbreak; especially when they come equipped with Ben & Jerry's.

# NOTES

# SECTION 6:

## THRIVING IN OUR DAILY LIVES

You are a powerful being. You wake up each morning, full of hopes and dreams, and do your best to make them a reality. It takes courage to tell a world that at times feels like it only wants you to fail, that you are going to try anyway. It's admirable. Even on those days when it feels like you've got nothing done, where your ability to convert oxygen into carbon dioxide feels like your biggest achievement, you still woke up in spite of it all. In a world that throws everything it can at us, don't be afraid to throw something back.

Finding ways to face your fears and dispel your doubts takes time and practice. You may not see the changes you desire happen overnight, but you will feel an immediate difference in your outlook when you change your mindset. You are always going to have worries about one thing or another. Letting those worries hold you back from going for what you want is the fastest way to fail. You destroy your chance before you can even take it. Determine how to assuage your fears and doubts before they are all that you have left.

Sometimes there are big moments in our lives that require a bit more support and encouragement than others: a wedding, the birth of a child, when it's your turn to read out loud in class and there is a word you aren't sure how to pronounce. These are the times when we must look into ourselves for strength, all while trying to appease that part of us which doubts our ability to succeed. Believe in yourself because it is your opinion of you that has the most impact on your well-being.

Most of our minds are consumed with thoughts of the future. We daydream about our romantic adventures, about the success we hope to achieve, about who we will be in the next 25 years. I am all for people striving for a brighter future, but I hope you also take the time to enjoy life now. It may seem strange to need reminding that life is meant to be enjoyed, but it is a fact that is easily forgotten in the midst of this chaotic world. If we are too focused on the things we've done and the things we haven't, we miss what is happening in the moment. The enjoyment of life should be felt as often as possible.

The last section of this collection gives us the push we need to become the best version of ourselves. With quotes that will help you start and end your day, increase your self-confidence, guide you through romance and the future, and provide tips for achieving success, this section has everything needed for strengthening your mental resilience. Take back control of your life and fully feel how great it is to be alive.

# Dealing With Our Fears and Doubts

*He is able, who thinks he is able.*

–Gautama, The Lord Buddha

Having fears and doubts, especially when it comes to our inner selves, is a rather unfortunate part of human existence. Yet, I find this quote to be the most successful way to counteract their effects. Nothing is more powerful than to believe that you can. And one certain way to get there is by visualizing yourself meeting the end goal.

There is a certain famous golf movie where in one of the final scenes the hero visualizes the way the ball will go before hitting it, and indeed, it goes exactly as he previewed it. This, in my opinion, is the perfect illustration of the success of visualization. It is more powerful than we think. It is a free gift, so why not give it a try and use it? So, believe in your abilities; there is no place for doubt in this game.

*Our greatest enemies, the ones we must fight most often, are within.*

–Thomas Paine

No doubt about it. We can be our own worst critics and enemies. I'm sure you've all heard the term self-sabotage. It all stems from our fears and doubts, usually about ourselves. Sound familiar? That whole "Am I good enough?" question, or the "I don't deserve it" affirmation is there in every human being. The answers all depend on how we feel about ourselves. And that is directly related to how much power we allow our fears and self-doubts to have over us. We could indeed treat them as enemies but, perhaps—like all good, successful diplomats—we need to approach them from a different angle.

While we keep awareness that they could become our enemies, we must use them as motivators, as allies, to strive to be better, to prove to ourselves that yes we are able, and to push ourselves forward. I deal with self-doubts often. I deal with fears often. And what makes me overcome them is thinking, "What would my life be if I let them take over?" It would be a complete nightmare. So, I think the opposite of whatever fear or doubt presents itself. That is how it gets canceled.

We need to transform our greatest inner fear into our strongest motivation. During the time I lived in New York as a renter, no matter how successful I was in my career, I feared homelessness, losing it all, and I always used that fear to push me forward, to motivate me to get up every morning and do everything possible not to let that fear come true. So, use your fears and self-doubts as a source of strength and determination, as your inner checks. After all, we owe it to ourselves to strive for our dreams and push past those fears and doubts.

*Our greatest glory is not in never failing, but in rising every time we fall.*

–Confucius

Let's go back to the concept of getting up after falling. This quote is here to remind us that even when facing our own worst fears and doubts, we must remain certain within ourselves that no matter how many times we fall, we must promise ourselves to get up. It's a powerful promise you can make to yourself as you walk into a scary situation. And it's a strong life jacket to hold on to during uncertain times.

Trying to live your life in avoidance of failure will lead to a very dull and sad existence. Go out there and fail. Then get up and do it all over again. And again. Once you get ten stamps on your failure punch card, you get a free cookie.

*Courage is resistance to fear, master of fear, not absence of fear.*

–Mark Twain

While fear can be a good deterrent to keep us safe from harm, we must recognize it in all of us as a survival aspect of our humanity. But there are times when we must push past it in order to achieve whatever goal we're after. So, yes, a courageous person isn't one who doesn't feel fear, but one who pushes past it. (Come on! You think Captain Sully wasn't afraid as he landed that plane on the Hudson river on that freezing January day?)

When facing scary situations, I ask myself, "What's the worst thing that can happen?" And then, I prepare for that by developing plans A, B, C, and D. Being prepared against the worst-case scenario is often a great way to push past our greatest fears and go after that important goal.

*Winners are not afraid of losing. But losers are.*

–Unknown

While at first this quote sounds like a cheap, cheesy thing a politician would say at a rally, if we re-read it carefully, it has great meaning. It goes back to our reflection on the risks of being alive. Before going after a goal we've set for ourselves, we must be aware that there is a risk of loss. Winners know it's indeed a possibility but go forward anyway, obviously giving it their best. The others will be held back because they see the possibility of loss and won't move forward. So in this Matrix of life, the choice is yours: Will you take the red pill or the blue pill?

*When you doubt your power, you give power to your doubt.*

–Honoré de Balzac

No need to reflect on this one. It's straight and to the point.

# For the Beginning of the Day

*A life without feasts is like a long road without taverns.*

—Democritus

We get into our morning grooves and go about our day without thinking about what it means to actually live our lives. It's true that many of us are set in a life routine we cannot change, especially if married, a parent, or a caregiver. Where you rotate between the same five outfits, always use the same pump at the gas station, and would never dare to eat tacos for dinner if it weren't a Tuesday. Life shouldn't feel like Groundhog Day, where only the date on the calendar changes.

If you're in one of those routines where your day is just like the last one without any variety or change, make yourself a promise when you wake up tomorrow. Treat yourself to something you love that day, even if it's just for 30 minutes. Do something pleasant for yourself. Whether it's to sit under the sun for a few minutes in the quiet of the afternoon, treat yourself to that second scoop of ice cream, or have that glass of red wine at the end of your day. Put a pleasurable twist on your obligatory daily routine so it'll feel like you're living a little. You may even feel a little guilty. And that's ok. Nothing like a little guilty pleasure. When you promise yourself at the beginning of your day that you'll do something fun that day, it'll give you something to look forward to as you move through your obligations. In my opinion, it is those little moments of self-indulgence when we feel like we're really living life.

*We are shaped by our thoughts. We become what we think.*

–Gautama The Lord Buddha

Here I go again with the visualization concept, but I'm sure many of you agree that visualizing what we want, how we want it, right at the start of our day, truly sets our subconscious mind onto the path towards achieving that goal, whatever it is. So, let's make sure that as we wake up, our thoughts are positive. The subconscious mind can also make negative thoughts come true if we give them enough life inside our heads.

Doubts? Fears? Worries? Anytime they pop up, think exactly the opposite of that thought. For example, sometimes, when I'm on the highway, my fear throws a thought in my head about possible accidents. Right away, I imagine myself arriving home at the end of the day, parking in my usual spot, having arrived safe and sound (despite all the traffic). Counteract your negative thoughts with the total opposite. Soon you'll train your mind to stay within what I call "the light." No dark thoughts. Never feed them. (Especially after midnight. They're like Gremlins.)

*The secret of getting ahead is getting started.*

–Mark Twain

Why is this the hardest part? Especially on those days you don't feel like getting out of bed? When you wish you could hide under the covers and stay in all day? But it's like going to the dentist, or paying taxes, or having to sing a song at your best friend's karaoke party despite not being able to carry a tune even if it were strapped to your back. You just have to do it. Look to this little quote to start your engines and get to it.

# For the End of the Day

*Don't judge each day by the harvest you reap, but by the seed that you plant.*

–Robert Louis Stevenson

How was your day? Did you take those small steps toward meeting your long-term goal? Was it one of those days where you were putting out fires all day? No chance to work on those long-term goals? If you did not, take at least 20 minutes to work on one of them before going to bed. 20 minutes is better than zero minutes, and you'll feel better. It's good advice that a very successful and highly disciplined friend gave me, and I treasure it like a good gift. So I'm sharing it with you here. 20 minutes. Per day. It doesn't feel like much but, in the long term, it'll make a difference.

*Happiness will never come to those who fail to appreciate what they already have.*

–Gautama, The Lord Buddha

As we look back to the end of our day and take stock of it, it's important to be grateful— even if it was filled with challenges. I read somewhere that gratitude invites more to our lives, more of whatever it is we are grateful for.

As you lie back in bed, eyes closed, spend a minute on gratitude. Appreciate the air in your lungs, the shoes on your feet, the pile of books on your nightstand that you said you get around to reading one day but haven't. Take the time to enjoy what's yours.

# On Romance

*When words fail, music speaks.*

–William Shakespeare

What would romance be without music? In my opinion, it's a must. It's why people have songs that are 'theirs', why your heart swells to the melody as two lovers kiss for the first time in a movie, why your pulse quickens when you hear the jingle of the ice cream man. Music speaks to the deepest parts of your soul.

In an article titled "The Neurochemistry of Music," published in the journal, Trends in Cognitive Sciences, it is stated that "music is widely regarded, among other things, as a system for emotional communication" (Mona Lisa Chanda & Levitin, 2013). The article goes in-depth on how the effect of music in certain neurotransmitters of the brain can enhance or improve a person's mood overall, since it's shown to affect the dopamine centers positively. And when it comes to romance, another dopamine enhancer, music can be a major factor, no doubt about it. So, never fail to use it as the soundtrack to your great romance.

*A person's tongue can give you the taste of his heart.*

–Ibn Qayyim Al Jawziyyah

Romance and courtship are supposed to be the time when we are on our best behavior. So, listen to what the object of your desire says. Really listen. At times, what the object of our desire utters can be a romance killer. Don't overlook it, especially if you're going to give your heart and soul to this potential significant other.

*When one is in love, one begins by deceiving one's self, and one always ends by deceiving others. That is what the world calls romance.*

–Oscar Wilde

It starts off small. You fool yourself into thinking you actually like watching UFC fights, then it's thinking you don't mind living outside of the city. Then you look at the soft, contented smile of your partner and realize you'd do it all again. It's true that romance can be like a drug to some of us and, yes, we will likely lie to ourselves, but let's just be aware and enjoy it anyway.

*If one really loves a woman, all other women in the world become absolutely meaningless to one.*

–Oscar Wilde

Amen to that. And in my opinion, if that lasts a lifetime, or at least the time you spend with that person, that is true romance.

# On the Future

*Forever—is composed of nows.*

–Emily Dickinson

W hat we are doing right now, at this moment, will very likely influence our future. And look at you, you're reading this book! What a bright future awaits you.

*Twenty years from now you will be more disappointed by the things that you didn't do than the ones you did do.*

–Mark Twain

How many of us look back in regret for the things we didn't say or the things we didn't do at a particular moment in the past? They cycle through our minds, keeping us up at night, disrupting our showers, making it impossible to focus on the Daily Double clue of Jeopardy. And while it is easy to fall into that nasty little habit of regretting the past, we have the present to change that and do away with future regrets.

I remember once when I had gotten a promotion as Operations Executive at a very glamorous department store on the upper east side of Manhattan, a job that, at the time, I considered to be my dream. At 23, I felt like I had achieved one of my major career goals. I was due to start my new position as a big cheese of the entire Home Furnishings Division on January 1st, which was the same week my family had planned a trip to see loved ones we hadn't seen in years. And what did my 23-year-old ambitious self do? I chose my new job over that once- in-a-lifetime family gathering. Of course, I didn't know that at the time. I felt it would look bad to ask for that week off as I was due to start my new position.

As members of the family who had participated in that gathering got older and started dying, I realized what a lost opportunity that was to sit at the large family table, sharing a meal and much laughter together. What I would give to do as they did back in that January when I chose career over family. It's one of the things I will always regret. My career in that super-glamorous retail store eventually came to an end, as I moved on to more grown-up things. Yet, the family factor has been always present. Only that moment in time that I missed never happened again. As I've gotten older, I've kept that experience in mind. Careers come and go, but family—as imperfect and dysfunctional as it can be— is forever. So, yes, this is one of my major regrets. Thankfully there are not many after that, for I learned to be bolder in life.

# On Striving for Success

*I'm a great believer in luck, and I find the harder I work, the more I have of it.*

–Thomas Jefferson

There is no substitute for being out there and doing what it takes to get the job done. There will be times when we'll be tempted to cut corners or overlook details but, by doing that, we're sacrificing quality, the kind that makes a successful product. It's true, while luck can happen in certain situations in life (or lucky coincidences), we cannot count on that every time, especially to get us out of trouble. So, don't count on luck; count on yourself doing all that it takes. If lucky breaks come along, then that's just the icing on the cake. As a salesperson, I remember there were days when I did not feel like getting out there. Perhaps it was due to bad weather, mental exhaustion, or simply not being motivated, but whenever I forced myself to get out there, regardless of how I felt, it always turned out that something good happened. Like on snow days, when most doctor offices were less busy and few reps would show up, some of the busiest doctors had more time to sit down, talk, and get to know each other. I think, deep down, those doctors developed a respect for the committed reps who were out there no matter what. When the weather was good and offices were full again, guess which rep they wanted to see first?

*We are what we repeatedly do. Excellence, therefore, is not an act, but a habit.*

–Aristotle

Mmm… based on that premise, I'm a big cup of green tea latte with my cell phone in hand, hanging out under palm trees and listening to electronica. Those are three aspects present in my everyday life. All joking aside, I think we all understand the sentiment behind this quote but have trouble implementing it. I know it, yet I still don't make the time to get on that treadmill on a daily basis. I wish I did. But I do strive to do it. This is why this little quote has become a daily reminder in my electronic calendar as a personal life coach.

## *Don't cut corners with yourself.*

–Maria C Vale

I came to this conclusion as I got older, and it has now become my own personal quote. In my twenties, there were those times I'd come home after a party and be too tired to take the time to wash my face and remove my makeup, only to wake up berating myself for not doing it. We've all been there. But making it a habit isn't a good idea, not when our skin needs to breathe and reconstitute overnight as we sleep. (Otherwise, our face is going to look older than we are.)

Here's another example of cutting corners with ourselves: skipping our daily flossing. There's no doubt about it, flossing takes that extra step, those extra minutes, in front of the sink at the end of our day. When so much is demanding our attention, it's easy to let that minor little thing go, but as we all are reminded at the dentist's chair when our gums make us look like an extra in a slasher flick, it's something we cannot afford to forego since it will have terrible long-term health repercussions. So, I tell myself on a daily basis now, "It will only take 3 minutes." And 3 minutes I can do. After all, when you floss daily, it doesn't take long.

During my days as a busy pharma rep running to 7 a.m. meetings an hour away, I'd microwave my oatmeal, which I barely had the time to eat, and drink a diet soda along the way for energy. For years, it was a terrible habit. Then, five years later, I was diagnosed with cancer. I'm not saying each of those items caused it, for it's theorized cancer is caused by many factors, not just one, but when we're not careful about what we put in our bodies or how we care for it on a daily basis, it's going to show up sooner or later. I was cutting corners, often, with myself.

We have to make the time for all these minor, inconvenient details of our daily lives. There is a saying I heard somewhere that says that after age 40 our body presents us with the proverbial invoice. While it's necessary at times to cut corners with ourselves, making it a habit will show up in the long run. No one else can do these things for us but ourselves. And we're worth it.

# On the Enjoyment of Life

*In all things of nature, there is something of the marvelous.*

–Aristotle

Yes, there is "something of the marvelous" in nature and under the right circumstances, just being in its presence has soothing properties. I find that heading out to the beach to watch the sunrise is my personal church. Find your church in nature. Henry David Thoreau was on to something when he went to the woods. I recall my early days in college when I spent one semester in a well- known school on the Upper East Side of Manhattan. While going through the growing pains of experiencing adulthood—feeling like an extra on Gossip Girl with all its burdens and challenges—I used to sneak out to Central Park in between classes and sit by one of the rocks by the pond. What a difference it would make in my mindset. I'd return to the next class feeling as if I had been to a very relaxing spa. Things felt differently from only an hour before. It's like magic, the transforming magic of being around nature.

If you are ever feeling jaded, numb, like nothing can touch your emotions, take yourself out somewhere where nature is the predominant presence, like the mountains or the ocean. And if you can't go that far, take yourself to a local park. There is a soothing feeling that being around nature brings, especially if our hearts are uneasy. Literally sit under a tree if you can, perhaps next to some sort of body of water. Personally, I find the presence of water to be soothing. What about you? Find what works for you.

*Without music, life would be a mistake.*

–Friedrich Nietzsche

Especially if your life is full of stress. You saw this quote on the segment about dealing with the constant stream of negative news because I view it as an important elixir to counteract that. But I believe the presence of music is key to every aspect of life. Now, I'm sure some of you reading this book, or listening, may not be the musical type and don't think much of the presence of music in your lives. You may even view music as a sign of all play and certainly not related to serious work.

But today, more than ever, there is a growing body of scientific studies focusing on the effect music has, not only on the mental well-being of humans but also on the physical aspect. (Not to mention its effect on animals and plants!)

According to the article, "The Effect of Music on the Human Stress Response", published in the Public Library of Science project and featuring a study on the very topic, they concluded that "music listening impacted the psychobiological stress system" and that "these findings may help better understand the beneficial effects of music on the human body" (Thoma et al., 2013). If music is not a part of your daily routine, try to incorporate it, whether on the drive home, going out for a walk, or as you wait impatiently in front of the convection oven for your leftovers to reheat. You may have a favorite genre or, if you're not into music, I'd say start with classical or jazz until you find a genre that resonates with the inner you.

The idea behind using music to deal with life's stresses goes beyond the simple enjoyment of it, but also its power as a background de- stressor. Of course, music is like food; in order to consume it, it would help if you enjoyed it. So, find your favorite genre, build a playlist, and allow yourself to mentally escape in ways you haven't been able to before. Now, if you are a music lover, I don't need to tell you anything else. You understand how important it is to your life. In my case, I view music not only as an enjoyable aspect of life but as my personal life soundtrack. I bet many of you who enjoy music feel the same way.

*True happiness is to enjoy the present, without anxious dependence upon the future.*

–Seneca

Sometimes we need this quote to remind us to forget about the moments behind us. Or to stop worrying, at least for a moment, about what's yet to come. Instead, stay in the moment and enjoy the now. While it can be difficult to separate them, it's a worthwhile exercise that helps us to enjoy the present in its entirety, worry-free.

It seems like an easy and simple concept, but for some of us— worrywarts, control freaks, anxiety-riddled stress cases—it is not. But it's certainly worth the try. Besides, if I'm constantly worried about what could go wrong, how am I ever going to enjoy jumping head-first out of this skydiving plane?

*Joy is not in things; it is in us.*

–Richard Wagner

So true. Ask yourself, are you the glass-half-full person? Or the other? You don't have to answer that to anyone but yourself. Some people are wired one way and some are wired another, but there is something to be said about always looking to find the best in every situation, even in the midst of an emotional hell storm. It keeps our outlook positive and helps us remain resilient. So, if you're the glass-half-empty kind of person, chances are you're thinking nothing can help you. But try some of the things I've mentioned above this quote, such as heading out to be in the middle of nature or listening to music that makes you happy. Start with that.

So, will I find joy in owning the limited edition of every Penguin Classics novel to display on my bookshelf? Perhaps for a short time. Will I find joy in being a good friend, taking care of myself, and making peace with the parts of me that I have difficulty accepting? Endlessly.

***

*Walk away from anything or anyone who takes away from your joy. Life is too short to put up with fools.*

–Unknown

As we reach the final quotes of this book, there is no doubt this is one that needs to be etched into our minds. While it is easy to walk away from people and situations that are not in our inner circle, the hardest part is to pull away from those who are. They could be close members of our own family or a significant other. And while these reflections are not professional advice, if you need to find a way out of a situation that continuously makes you unhappy, no matter how much you try, I highly encourage you to hire yourself a professional advisor (something that kids these days call a 'therapist') and together find a way.

Let's hope that whatever way you decide—music, therapy, music therapy, or even starting your own collection of reflective quotes—ends up working for you. If anything, we owe it to ourselves to be happy. It's the one thing we have control over. That's right. While others can make you happy, that's only a temporary situation. The whole permanent happiness concept is really up to each of us.

***

*He is a wise man who does not grieve for the things which he has not, but rejoices for those which he has.*

–Epictetus

Whether that's the body you wish you had or that limited edition of The Beatles' Yesterday and Today vinyl record someone just outbid you for on eBay, there is no gain in sulking over the things you don't have.

This is all about gratitude. It is no secret that the way to abundance and success is being grateful for the things we have, perfect or not. Crazy, you may think, but after our latest pandemic, something as simple as being able to breathe is something to be thankful for (and toilet paper!). So, let's not forget to count our blessings when we wake up and before we go to bed. I have found the more grateful I am, the more opportunities I encounter. Have you?

*In the end, it's not the years in your life that count. It's the life in your years.*

–Abraham Lincoln

I want to end this collection of favorite shareable quotes with this one. As simple as the concept may be, it's so easy to forget. For many years I took life for granted. I dreamt of what I would like to achieve as I got older and even into my golden years, living in a house by the water and writing books. I took it for granted that I would get there someday. But being diagnosed with cancer in my late thirties changed that mindset, especially when I realized that I may not make it to those golden years. So I had to accelerate those long-term plans, and started by moving to Florida, finding that house by the water I always envisioned, and writing this book.

The truth is that I have found happiness living a simpler lifestyle here, one I always wanted, where I strive to do something fun and joyful under the sun on a daily basis. My life is not perfect but is one that makes me happy. In a way, this diagnosis woke me up from my corporate life in the concrete jungle, where I encountered a lot of negative stress which eventually forced me out. So, I say to you, don't wait for a life-changing diagnosis or some other traumatic event to force change upon you. Take this book, these quotes, and my reflections as your sign to make those changes for yourself. It is the life you put in your years that makes life worth living, however long you may have, so do what you need to do to achieve that. You are worth the happiness that only you can bring to yourself.

# NOTES

# AFTERWORD

A nd so, we have come to the end of this sharing journey. As your host in this book, I can only hope your experience has been one where you feel empowered and less stressed about your daily life challenges.

When I decided to put together this collection of quotes and share it with readers like you, it wasn't because I have a perfect life and have made it to the top of the proverbial mountain. It's because we are all in this together. We all face challenges along our life paths. No one has a perfect life. Even my friends who are wealthier, more successful, and better looking than me have to deal with their daily annoying challenges. We all do. Never doubt that.

This book was more about sharing the experiences, struggles, and goals we have in common and how this fellow human is dealing with them. To this day, I continue to face difficult situations and, while sometimes I strike out, it is the daily quotes that pop up in my calendar that keep me focused to hit those home runs. And I've hit enough of them to feel that the challenging moments were worth it. It is those wins in life, especially when going against the odds, against the naysayers who said it couldn't be done, that make life fun and worth getting up every morning. No doubt we all thrive on that!

I recall in my early adulthood days, looking for answers about certain aspects of life on the shelves of my college library. And I will always remain grateful to those writers, many of them long gone, who put thoughts and experiences to paper and made me realize that this whole human experience is universal. Someone out there has already thought it, felt it, done it, feared it, experienced it, hated it, and loved it. We are not alone in our humanity. And finding that out lifted a big weight from my young and scared shoulders.

In a way, this book is about paying it forward. Maybe someone will find this book one day on some library shelf, and it will help them the way those books did for me in my younger days when I had so many questions about life, people, and situations.

There are many more quotes, aphorisms, and truisms out there. I hope the ones in this book resonated with you. I invite you to make them your own. I also have no doubt that you already have your own favorites. I encourage you to continue to build your own set throughout your life, and use them as your little hacks to mental resilience. I urge you to put them in your calendar or whatever place your eyes rest often. We all need those mental markers to reset us. We all need those coaching pointers to keep us steady through our days. If you want to share which are your favorites and why, I'd be thrilled for you to visit my social pages listed below. I'd love to hear from you about your thoughts on this collection, how it may have helped you, and which quotes you'll be adding to your daily rotation.

Thank you again for taking this journey with me, now it's your turn to reflect.

For any live feedback on this work, I invite you to connect with me on my website and socials, share your experiences, and look for updates:

Website: http://mariacvaleproductions.com

Facebook:   https://www.facebook.com/mcvalebooks/

Twitter:       @MCValeBooks

Reddit: r/mcvalebooks

Instagram: @mcvalebooks

Tik Tok: mcvalebooks

If you have enjoyed this book, I would be appreciative if you left a review on the book listing page so that potential readers have an idea of what to expect. As a new author, your responses and reviews are hugely important. These first reviews are paramount to an author's success and survival in the rankings. So, in advance, I thank you for taking the time.

# WITH GRATITUDE

I used to always say, "I owe who I am to God, my mother, and Bloomingdale's." A decade or so later, I added Pfizer. Today the list is a little longer. So, while I won't bore you my friends, with the long list of people, places, and things I'm grateful for in life, I do feel it is worthwhile to acknowledge the people, situations, and things that have helped me write and publish this book. Those who are referenced here have, in some other way or another, contributed directly or indirectly to this work and its publication.

To my mother, yes, the lady who up to this day causes me, (at times) to roll my eyes, when giving me unsolicited advice, and with whom at times I disagree. Yes, you, Mama. Despite that, I am always grateful for the lessons you taught me; to be positive, to push past fears, to do the improbable. When the world is telling you that it can't be done, you always find a way. My brother and I saw that, watched you break barriers, do the impossible, and learned. Thank you for those lessons. Thank you for your sacrifices and examples in courage, creativity, and always finding a way in the darkest moments. And, especially, thank you for being there those long days and nights in the hospitals when I was seriously ill. Those times you mentally pulled me up, when I was ready to let the cancer win, and you whispered in my ear, "No, it's not your time." Yes, I know none of us are perfect, but I remain always grateful to you for all you're doing, and you've done. And I hope I can count on you to help me with the Spanish version of this book, when the Spanish dichos, your way, are shared with the world. One day the world will know your story too. It deserves to be told.

To my three favorite former employers: Bloomingdale's, Pfizer, and Verizon Wireless. It was during my time at each of these companies that I continued to develop my collection of quotes and success principles. Interesting how these employers all touched a decade of my professional life, and more importantly, they had such an impact on my psyche, not only as a career professional but as a human being. There I met some of the most amazing people, some who remain in my life up to this day. While I'm grateful for the great experience, the paychecks, and the perks, I am most grateful for the awesome friends, coworkers, mentors, and managers who crossed my path, from whom I learned, and many who are in my circle today, and for whom I'm so grateful and honored to know.

To the amazing friends in my life and even those of you who have moved on. Thank you! Each of you has taught me something, and often something reminds me of you, even though we may not be in touch as much, or anymore, or distance has stretched our bond.

Ronnie Jordan, my dear. Thank you for always replying to my texts asking you the silliest questions as I was about to publish this book. You are my trusted light in this new path of book publishing. I'm so grateful for your patient friendship and constant encouragement.

Shelby Ripka, my highly disciplined friend, from whom I often draw inspiration to do better and be better. The 20-minute-a-day advice I always take to heart, as well as the "checks and balances" concept. Thank you!

My beloved friend and former teammate from my Pfizer days, Joy Washington. You certainly brought me much joy, working side by side, and taught me unforgettable lessons in human relations and overcoming, even in the face of adversity and improbability. I love how you keep succeeding despite whatever obstacle shows up in your path. I'm your biggest cheerleader, even from afar. We succeeded despite it all!

A big thanks to that tough-but-fair Pfizer manager, Fran Barnette, who at times stressed me out, but also did a hell of a job motivating me. You did challenge us to do better, and in the end, you rewarded us for bringing home the results. You were my first sales-career manager, and you left your mark in my style. Thank you for the lessons.

Scott Burrows, the quiet guy who didn't say much at those boisterous sales meetings, but certainly set the example for us by staying #1 year after year. Thank you for the lessons and for your friendship.

To my dear friend and adopted big sister, Linda Burgos. Thank you for always being there for me, like that day at the traffic ticket court in NJ when I knew you were hoping I wouldn't say anything to piss off the judge. For the time you were there for me when my car got towed, when I needed that ride to the ER late at night, so you drove all the way from NJ. For when you helped me pack and move. I will always be grateful and can only hope that even with how much I will try to repay you, more of that well-deserved good karma will show up in your path.

To my dear friend and wise guru, Dee Sabers. Thank you for your support and interest in this project, and for being a great listener and sounding board. I always value your advice, and your open door.

To my darling little bro, Javier, my beloved sibling, with whom I've shared so much. We've had our ups and downs, but the ups are multiple times greater, and I'm so grateful we've been friends and partners in crime and good deeds throughout our lives. Thank you for being my cheerleader when I least expected it and for being so supportive when I could turn to no one else. Cheers to the "Hermanos Kent!" And cheers to your beautiful family. I love you guys!

A big thanks to my amazing doctors and nurses, who've helped me stay alive this long. You've been my partners in survival, especially the awesome Dr. Kathy Crew at Columbia Presbyterian, for not giving up on me; for helping me find the way out of the scariest moments; for always letting me make the final decisions; for respecting me as a patient. Thank you for walking in when I needed an oncologist and was too scared to find one. You have been my angel through the unexpectedly long years.

To my fabulous vascular doc, Dr. Celestin of the Cleveland Clinic, Florida. You totally get me and have helped me walk the fine line of controlling my situation. I will continue to drive the hour just to go see you, and I only hope you don't go farther than that, or I'll have to drive longer or take a plane.

To my no-nonsense, super cool PCP, Dr. Galante, in West Palm Beach. I fear you as much as I love you, so I always try to watch my sugar and cheese intake the weeks before seeing you, or you will read me the riot act. I love how you keep me in line, healthy, and always find an answer to my health questions in that loving, funny but tough way. Don't ever change or ever lose Sandy, that awesome assistant of yours, who's miraculous and makes things happen.

Last, but not least, my oncologist here in South Florida, the fantastic Dr. Reshma Mahtani, from Miami University Hospital and Baptist Health South Florida. I got so lucky finding you. You also get me and respect me as a patient. Thank you for guiding me and treating me as an equal when discussing my situation. I enjoy our visits and feel safe being treated by you. There's no doubt you know your specialty well. I love your super informative sessions on video! I hope you and Dr. Crew meet one day. You two deserve to know each other.

I feel so lucky to be in the hands of these amazing doctors. They are my partners in health and survival. And I'm grateful to each of them and their support teams, especially the awesome nurses in the oncology group in those institutions, who make it all happen. Thanks to their good care, I am still around so I can write this book today.

One more name many of you may not know, and that's Penelope, from the Urban Writers team, who helped me get organized with this book and helped me move it forward to a publishable format. Even though I have a BA in English, with a writing concentration, and love to write, I did not have the professional discipline to have put this book into a format ready to publish. So, I'm grateful to Penelope's help and guidance, with whom I worked closely, who got me, and the spirit behind this book.

I could go on naming quite a few more of you here, but I fear that when naming names I could leave someone out, but there is always the next book. 😊

Lastly, I'm not a religious kind of girl, but I am grateful to God, St. Jude, and all the good spirits for helping keep me alive, safe, and sound all this time. The miraculous turnarounds I've witnessed have made me a believer. I am grateful. Always grateful.

'Till the next book.

# INTERESTED IN BUYING 10 OR MORE COPIES?

# OR FOR SPEAKING ENGAGEMENTS

# WRITE TO ME

**info@mariacvaleproductions.com**

# References

Avildsen, J. G. (Director). (1984). *The Karate Kid*. Columbia Pictures.

Chumbawamba. (1997). *Tubthumping*. EMI.

Dante, J. (Director). (1984). *Gremlins*. Warner Bros.

Griffin, M. (1964). *Jeopardy*. NBC.

Hole, J., Hirsch, M., Ball, E., & Meads, C. (2015). *Music as an aid for postoperative recovery in adults: a systematic review and meta- analysis*. The Lancet, 386(10004), 1659–1671. https://doi.org/10.1016/s0140-6736(15)60169-6

Jones, D., & Daily, M. (1997). *Grand Theft Auto*. Sony Computer Entertainment., Rockstar North., & Rockstar Games (Firm).

Lee, S., & Ditko, S. (1962). *Amazing Fantasy Vol. 15*. Marvel. http://marvel.com/comics/issue/16926/amazing_fantasy_1962_15

Lincoln, A., Epictetus, Wagner, R., Seneca, Nietzsche, F., Aristotle, Jefferson, T., Twain, M., Dickinson, E., Al Jawziyyah, I. Q., Shakespeare, W., Guatama, Stevenson, R. L., de Balzac, H., Confucius, Paine, T., Austen, J., Bruno, G., Best-Quotations Home Page. Best Quotations. Retrieved September 11, 2021, from https://best-quotations.com

Martin, G. R. R. (1996). A Game of Thrones. Bantam Books.

Meyer, S. (2005). Twilight. Little, Brown and Company.

Mona Lisa Chanda, & Levitin, D. J. (2013). The neurochemistry of music. Trends in Cognitive Sciences, 17(4), 179–193. https://doi.org/10.1016/j.tics.2013.02.007

Pearlman, M. (2009). Chopped. Food Network.

Persson, M., Bergensten, J., & McManus, S. (2009). Minecraft. Mojang Studios., Xbox Game Studios., Sony Interactive Entertainment., & Telltale Games.

Rowling, J. K. (1997). Harry Potter and the Sorcerer's Stone. Scholastic Inc.

Simon & Schuster, https://www.simonandschuster.com/books/How-To-Win-Friends-and-Influence-People/Dale-Carnegie/9781439167342

Thoma, M. V., La Marca, R., Brönnimann, R., Finkel, L., Ehlert, U., & Nater, U. M. (2013). The Effect of Music on the Human Stress Response. PLoS ONE, 8(8), e70156. https://doi.org/10.1371/journal.pone.0070156

Tolkien, J. R. R. (1954). The Fellowship of the Ring. Allen & Unwin.

Tzu, Sun. (5th Century BC). The Art of War (L. Giles, Trans.) classics.mit.edu/Tzu/artwar.html

Wachowski, L., & Wachowski, L. (Directors). (1999). The Matrix. Warner Bros.

Wallis, J. S. (2019). Tidying Up with Marie Kondo. Netflix.

Wilde, O. (2013). Complete works of Oscar Wilde. Hardpress Publishing.

Wright, E., & Cornish, J. (Directors). (2015). Ant-Man. Marvel Studios.

Zacconi, R. (2012). Candy Crush. King.

www.ingramcontent.com/pod-product-compliance
Lightning Source LLC
Chambersburg PA
CBHW060520130626
46553CB00002B/581

* 9 7 9 8 9 8 5 3 4 9 6 0 3 *